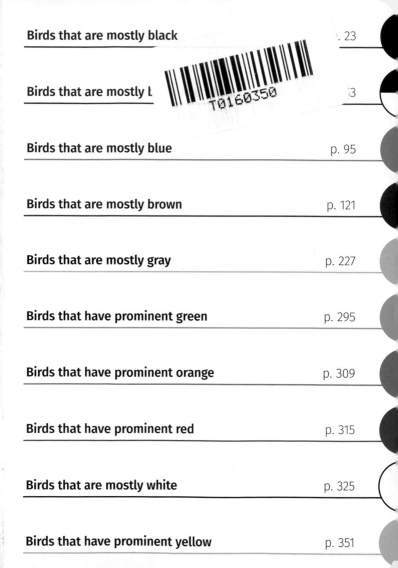

T0160350

# Birds *of* Florida

## Field Guide

Stan Tekiela

Adventure Publications
Cambridge, Minnesota

## Dedication

To my wife, Katherine, and daughter, Abigail, with all my love.

## Acknowledgments

Special thanks to the National Wildlife Refuge System, which stewards the land that is critical to many bird species. Thanks also to Bill Pranty, Audubon of Florida, and Wes Biggs, President of Florida Nature Tours, for reviewing the range maps.

Edited by Sandy Livoti and Dan Downing

Cover, book design and illustrations by Jonathan Norberg

Range maps produced by Anthony Hertzel

**Cover photo: Painted Bunting by Stan Tekiela**
**All photos by Stan Tekiela** except p. 66 (breeding) by **Agami Photo Agency/Shutterstock**; p. 332 (juvenile) by **Rick and Nora Bowers**; pp. 186 (displaying), 224 (juvenile and chick-feeding adult) and 276 (displaying) by **Dudley Edmondson**; p. 238 (winter) by **FotoRequest/Shutterstock**; p. 228 by **Frode Jacobsen/Shutterstock**; pp. 42 (soaring), 86 (main) and 240 (winter) by **Kevin T. Karlson**; p. 286 (in flight) by **Brian E Kushner/Shutterstock**; p. 76 (in flight) by **Brian Lasenby/Shutterstock**; p. 328 (breeding) by **David Osborn/Shutterstock**; p. 152 (breeding) by **Paul Reeves Photography/Shutterstock**; p. 42 (drying) by **JayPierstorff/Shutterstock**; p. 154 (breeding) **Brian E. Small**; p. 262 (displaying) by **Harmut Walter**; pp. 42 (juvenile), 44 (juvenile), 164 (both juveniles), 278 (juvenile) and 282 (in-flight juvenile) by **Brian K. Wheeler**; and pp. 210 (female), 270 (main), 324 (main) and 352 (female) by **Jim Zipp**

To the best of the publisher's knowledge, all photos were of live birds. Some were photographed in a controlled condition.

15  14  13  12  11  10  9  8
**Birds of Florida Field Guide**
First Edition 2001, Second Edition 2004
Third Edition 2020
Copyright © 2001, 2004 and 2020 by Stan Tekiela
Published by Adventure Publications
An imprint of AdventureKEEN
310 Garfield Street South
Cambridge, Minnesota 55008
(800) 678-7006
www.adventurepublications.net
All rights reserved
Printed in China
ISBN 978-1-64755-065-3 (pbk.); ISBN 978-1-64755-066-0 (ebook)

# TABLE OF CONTENTS

## WHAT'S NEW?

It is hard to believe that it's been more than 15 years since the debut of *Birds of Florida Field Guide*. This critically acclaimed field guide has helped countless people identify and enjoy the birds that we love. Now, in this expanded third edition, *Birds of Florida Field Guide* has many new and exciting changes and a fresh look, while retaining the same familiar, easy-to-use format.

To help you identify even more birds in Florida, I have added 9 new species and more than 150 new color photographs. All of the range maps have been meticulously reviewed, and many updates have been made to reflect the ever-changing movements of the birds.

Everyone's favorite section, "Stan's Notes," has been expanded to include even more natural history information. "Compare" sections have been updated to help ensure that you correctly identify your bird, and additional feeder information has been added to help with bird feeding. I hope you will enjoy this great new edition as you continue to learn about and appreciate our Florida birds!

# WHY WATCH BIRDS IN FLORIDA?

Millions of people have discovered bird feeding. It's a simple and enjoyable way to bring the beauty of birds closer to your home. Watching the birds at your feeder and listening to them often leads to a lifetime pursuit of bird identification. The *Birds of Florida Field Guide* is for those who want to identify the common birds of Florida.

There are over 1,100 species of birds found in North America. In Florida alone there have been more than 500 different kinds of birds recorded through the years. That is an impressive amount of birds for a single state! These bird sightings were diligently recorded by hundreds of bird watchers and became part of the official state record. From these valuable records, I have chosen 146 of the most common and easily seen birds of Florida to include in this field guide.

Bird watching, often called birding, is one of the most popular activities in America. Its outstanding appeal in Florida is due, in part, to an unusually rich and abundant birdlife. Why are there so many birds in this state? One reason is water, both saltwater and fresh. Peninsular Florida is surrounded by water and has 1,350 miles (2,175 km) of coastline. It's home to many ocean-loving birds such as the colony-nesting Royal Tern and surf-running Sanderling. In addition to the coast, Florida has thousands of sizable lakes such as Lake Okeechobee—the eighth largest lake in the U.S.—thousands of freshwater and saltwater marshes, not to mention four major rivers. All of this water attracts millions of birds such as the Tricolored Heron and Roseate Spoonbill.

Climate is another reason why Florida has so many birds. The northern part of Florida is classified as humid subtropical, while southern Florida is considered tropical wet, more typical of Central America. The relatively warm climate affords birds extra time to raise more than one brood per season, or to feed unimpeded during severe winters elsewhere.

Southern Florida not only attracts people to its warm winter climate, it is also a winter home to hundreds of migratory bird species. From tiny birds, such as the Palm and Black-and-white Warblers, to the Ruddy Turnstone, an ornately colored shorebird that nests in coastal Alaska, millions of birds pack into southern Florida each winter to feed in the state's nutrient-rich waters and fertile forests.

While water and weather are good reasons for a vast abundance of birds in Florida, keep in mind the great size of the state. Florida is the twenty-second largest state, covering approximately 65,755 square miles (170,300 sq. km), about 50 percent of which is covered with forest. Florida's forests are home to such birds as the Chuck-will's-widow, whose calls throughout the night can be heard each spring and summer.

Florida is one of the best places in North America to see a wide array of birds. Whether witnessing a nesting colony of herons and egrets in the Everglades or welcoming back the wintering shorebirds, bird watchers enjoy variety and excitement in Florida as each season turns to the next.

## OBSERVE WITH A STRATEGY; TIPS FOR IDENTIFYING BIRDS

Identifying birds isn't as difficult as you might think. By simply following a few basic strategies, you can increase your chances of successfully identifying most birds that you see. One of the first and easiest things to do when you see a new bird is to note its **color**. This field guide is organized by color, so simply turn to the right color section to find it.

Next, note the **size of the bird.** A strategy to quickly estimate size is to compare different birds. Pick a small, a medium and a large bird. Select an American Robin as the medium bird.

Measured from bill tip to tail tip, a robin is 10 inches (25 cm). Now select two other birds, one smaller and one larger. Good choices are a House Sparrow, at about 6 inches (15 cm), and an American Crow, around 18 inches (45 cm). When you see a species you don't know, you can now quickly ask yourself, "Is it larger than a sparrow but smaller than a robin?" When you look in your field guide to identify your bird, you would check the species that are roughly 6–10 inches (15–25 cm). This will help to narrow your choices.

Next, note the **size, shape and color of the bill.** Is it long or short, thick or thin, pointed or blunt, curved or straight? Seed-eating birds, such as Northern Cardinals, have bills that are thick and strong enough to crack even the toughest seeds. Birds that sip nectar, such as Ruby-throated Hummingbirds, need long, thin bills to reach deep into flowers. Hawks and owls tear their prey with very sharp, curving bills. Sometimes, just noting the bill shape can help you decide whether the bird is a woodpecker, finch, blackbird or bird of prey.

Next, take a look around and note the **habitat** in which you see the bird. Is it wading in a saltwater marsh? Walking along a riverbank or on the beach? Soaring in the sky? Is it perched high in the trees or hopping along the forest floor? Because of diet and habitat preferences, you'll often see robins hopping on the ground but not usually eating seeds at a feeder. Or you'll see a Blue Jay sitting on a tree branch but not climbing headfirst down the trunk, like a Brown-headed Nuthatch would.

Noticing **what the bird is eating** will give you another clue to help you identify the species. Feeding is a big part of any bird's life. Fully one-third of all bird activity revolves around searching for food, catching prey and eating. While birds don't always follow all the rules of their diet, you can make some general assumptions. Northern Flickers, for instance, feed on ants and other insects, so you wouldn't expect to see them visiting a seed feeder. Other birds, such as Barn and Tree Swallows, eat flying insects and spend hours swooping and diving to catch a meal.

Sometimes you can identify a bird by **the way it perches.** Body posture can help you differentiate between an American Crow and a Red-tailed Hawk, for example. Crows lean forward over their feet on a branch, while hawks perch in a vertical position. Consider posture the next time you see an unidentified large bird in a tree.

Birds in flight are harder to identify, but noting the **wing size and shape** will help. Wing size is in direct proportion to body size, weight and type of flight. Wing shape determines whether the bird flies fast and with precision, or slowly and less precisely. Barn Swallows, for instance, have short, pointed wings that slice through the air, enabling swift, accurate flight. Turkey Vultures have long, broad wings for soaring on warm updrafts. House Finches have short, rounded wings, helping them to flit through thick tangles of branches.

Some bird species have a unique **pattern of flight** that can help in identification. American Goldfinches fly in a distinctive undulating pattern that makes it look like they're riding a roller coaster.

While it's not easy to make all of these observations in the short time you often have to watch a "mystery" bird, practicing these identification methods will greatly expand your birding skills. To further improve your skills, seek the guidance of a more experienced birder who can answer your questions on the spot.

## BIRD BASICS

It's easier to identify birds and communicate about them if you know the names of the different parts of a bird. For instance, it's more effective to use the word "crest" to indicate the set of extra-long feathers on top of a Northern Cardinal's head than to try to describe it.

The following illustration points out the basic parts of a bird. Because it is a composite of many birds, it shouldn't be confused with any actual bird.

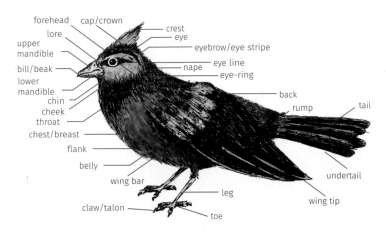

## Bird Color Variables

No other animal has a color palette like a bird's. Brilliant blues, lemon yellows, showy reds and iridescent greens are common in the bird world. In general, male birds are more colorful than their female counterparts. This helps males attract a mate, essentially saying, "Hey, look at me!" Color calls attention to a male's health as well. The better the condition of his feathers, the better his food source, territory and potential for mating.

Male and female birds that don't look like each other are called sexually dimorphic, meaning "two forms." Dimorphic females often have a nondescript dull color, as seen in Indigo Buntings. Muted tones help females hide during the weeks of motionless incubation and draw less attention to them when they're out feeding or taking a break from the rigors of raising the young.

The males of some species, such as the Downy Woodpecker, Blue Jay and Bald Eagle, look nearly identical to the females. In woodpeckers, the sexes are differentiated by only a red mark, or sometimes a yellow mark. Depending on the species, the mark may be on top of the head, on the face or nape of neck, or just behind the bill.

During the first year, juvenile birds often look like their mothers. Since brightly colored feathers are used mainly for attracting a mate, young non-breeding males don't have a need for colorful plumage. It's not until the first spring molt (or several years later, depending on the species) that young males obtain their breeding colors.

Both breeding and winter plumages are the result of molting. Molting is the process of dropping old, worn feathers and replacing them with new ones. All birds molt, typically twice a year, with the spring molt usually occurring in late winter. At this time, most birds produce their brighter breeding plumage, which lasts throughout the summer.

Winter plumage is the result of the late summer molt, which serves a couple of important functions. First, it adds feathers for warmth in the coming winter season. Second, in some species it produces feathers that tend to be drab in color, which helps to camouflage the birds and hide them from predators. The winter plumage of the male American Goldfinch, for example, is olive-brown, unlike its canary-yellow breeding color during summer. Luckily for us, some birds, such as the male Northern Cardinal, retain their bright summer colors all year long.

## Bird Nests

Bird nests are a true feat of engineering. Imagine constructing a home that's strong enough to weather storms, large enough to hold your entire family, insulated enough to shelter them from cold and heat, and waterproof enough to keep out rain. Think about building it without blueprints or directions and using mainly your feet. Birds do this!

Before building, birds must select an appropriate site. In some species, such as the House Wren, the male picks out several potential sites and assembles small twigs in each. The "extra" nests, called dummy nests, discourage other birds from using any nearby cavities for their nests. The male takes the female around and shows her the choices. After choosing her favorite, she finishes the construction.

In other species, such as the Baltimore Oriole, the female selects the site and builds the nest, while the male offers an occasional suggestion. Each bird species has its own nest-building routine that is strictly followed.

As you can see in these illustrations, birds build a wide variety of nest types.

**ground nest**  **platform nest**  **cup nest**  **pendulous nest**  **cavity nest**

Nesting material often consists of natural items found in the immediate area. Most nests consist of plant fibers (such as bark from grapevines), sticks, mud, dried grass, feathers, fur, or soft, fuzzy tufts from thistle. Some birds, including Ruby-throated Hummingbirds, use spiderwebs to glue nest materials together.

Transportation of nesting material is limited to the amount a bird can hold or carry. Birds must make many trips afield to gather enough material to complete a nest. Most nests take four days or more, and hundreds, if not thousands, of trips to build.

A **ground nest** can be a mound of vegetation on the ground or in water. It can also be just a simple, shallow depression scraped out in earth, stones or sand. Killdeer and Black Skimmers scrape out ground nests without adding any nesting material.

The **platform nest** represents a much more complex type of construction. Typically built with twigs or sticks and branches, this nest forms a platform and has a depression in the center to nestle the eggs. Platform nests can be in trees; on balconies, cliffs, bridges, or man-made platforms; and even in flowerpots. They often provide space for the adventurous young and function as a landing platform for the parents.

Mourning Doves and herons don't anchor their platform nests to trees, so these can tumble from branches during high winds and storms. Hawks, eagles, ospreys and other birds construct sturdier platform nests with large sticks and branches.

Other platform nests are constructed on the ground with mud, grass and other vegetation from the area. Many waterfowl build platform nests on the ground near or in water. A **floating platform nest** moves with the water level, preventing the nest, eggs and birds from being flooded.

Three-quarters of all songbirds construct a **cup nest,** which is a modified platform nest. The supporting platform is built first and attached firmly to a tree, shrub, or rock ledge or the ground. Next, the sides are constructed with grass, small twigs, bark or leaves, which are woven together and often glued with mud for added strength. The inner cup can be lined with down feathers, animal fur or hair, or soft plant materials and is contoured last.

The **pendulous nest** is an unusual nest that looks like a sock hanging from a branch. Attached to the end of small branches of trees, this unique nest is inaccessible to most predators and often waves wildly in a breeze.

Woven tightly with plant fibers, the pendulous nest is strong and watertight and takes up to a week to build. A small opening at the top or on the side allows parents access to the grass-lined interior. More commonly used by tropical birds, this complex nest has also been mastered by orioles and kinglets. It must be one heck of a ride to be inside one of these nests during a windy spring thunderstorm!

The **cavity nest** is used by many species of birds, most notably woodpeckers and Eastern Bluebirds. A cavity nest is often excavated from a branch or tree trunk and offers shelter from storms, sun, cold and predators. A small entrance hole in a tree can lead to a nest chamber that is up to a safe 10 inches (25 cm) deep.

Typically made by woodpeckers, cavity nests are usually used only once by the builder. Nest cavities can be used for many subsequent years by such inhabitants as Tree Swallows, mergansers and bluebirds. Kingfishers, on the other hand, can dig a tunnel up to 4 feet (1 m) long in a riverbank. The nest chamber at the end of the tunnel is already well insulated, so it's usually only sparsely lined.

One of the most clever of all nests is the **no nest,** or daycare nest. Parasitic birds, such as Brown-headed Cowbirds, don't build their own nests. Instead, the egg-laden female searches out the nest of another bird and sneaks in to lay an egg while the host mother isn't looking.

A mother cowbird wastes no energy building a nest only to have it raided by a predator. Laying her eggs in the nests of other birds transfers the responsibility of raising her young to the host. When she lays her eggs in several nests, the chances increase that at least one of her babies will live to maturity.

## Who Builds the Nest?

Generally, the female bird constructs the nest. She gathers the materials and does the building, with an occasional visit from her mate to check on progress. In some species, both parents contribute equally to nest building. The male may forage for sticks, grass or mud, but it is the female that often fashions the nest. Only rarely does a male build a nest by himself.

## Fledging

Fledging is the time between hatching and flight, or leaving the nest. Some species of birds are **precocial,** meaning they leave the nest within hours of hatching, though it may be weeks before they can fly. This is common in waterfowl and shorebirds.

Baby birds that hatch naked and blind need to stay in the nest for a few weeks (these birds are **altricial**). Baby birds that are still in the nest are **nestlings.** Until birds start to fly, they are called **fledglings.**

## Why Birds Migrate

Why do so many species of birds migrate? The short answer is simple: food. Birds migrate to locations with abundant food, as it is easier to breed where there is food than where food is scarce. Summer Tanagers, for instance, are **complete migrators** that fly from the tropics of South America to nest in the forests of North America, where billions of newly hatched insects are available to feed to their young.

Other migrators, such as some birds of prey, migrate back to northern regions in spring. In these locations, they hunt mice, voles and other small rodents that are beginning to breed.

Complete migrators have a set time and pattern of migration. Every year at nearly the same time, they head to a specific wintering ground. Complete migrators may travel great distances, sometimes 15,000 miles (24,100 km) or more in one year.

Complete migration doesn't necessarily mean flying from Florida to a tropical destination. Baltimore Orioles, for example, are complete migrators that move from southern states with mild winters, such as Tennessee and Mississippi, to spend winter here in Florida. This trip is still considered complete migration.

Complete migrators have many interesting aspects. In spring, males often leave a few weeks before the females, arriving early to scope out possibilities for nesting sites and food sources, and to begin to defend territories. The females arrive several weeks later. In many species, the females and their young leave earlier in the fall, often up to four weeks before the adult males.

Other species, such as the American Goldfinch, are **partial migrators**. These birds usually wait until their food supplies dwindle before flying south. Unlike complete migrators, partial migrators move only far enough south, or sometimes east and west, to find abundant food. In some years it might be only a few hundred miles, while in other years it can be as much as a thousand. This kind of migration, dependent on weather and the availability of food, is sometimes called seasonal movement.

Unlike the predictable complete migrators or partial migrators, **irruptive migrators** can move every third to fifth year or, in some cases, in consecutive years. These migrations are triggered when times are tough and food is scarce. Purple Finches are irruptive migrators. They leave their normal northern range in search of more food or in response to overpopulation.

Many other birds don't migrate at all. Carolina Chickadees, for example, are **non-migrators** that remain in their habitat all year long and just move around as necessary to find food.

## How Do Birds Migrate?

One of the many secrets of migration is fat. While most people are fighting the ongoing battle of the bulge, birds intentionally gorge themselves to gain as much fat as possible without losing the ability to fly. Fat provides the greatest amount of energy per unit of weight. In the same way that your car needs gas, birds are propelled by fat and stall without it.

During long migratory flights, fat deposits are used up quickly, and birds need to stop to refuel. This is when backyard bird feeding stations and undeveloped, natural spaces around our towns and cities are especially important. Some birds require up to 2–3 days of constant feeding to build their fat reserves before continuing their seasonal trip.

Many birds, such as most eagles, hawks, ospreys, falcons and vultures, migrate during the day. Larger birds can hold more body fat, go longer without eating and take longer to migrate. These birds glide along on rising columns of warm air, called thermals, that hold them aloft while they slowly make their way north or south. They generally rest at night and hunt early in the morning before the sun has a chance to warm the land and create good soaring conditions. Daytime migrators use a combination of landforms, rivers, and the rising and setting sun to guide them in the right direction.

The majority of small birds, called **passerines,** migrate at night. Studies show that some use the stars to navigate. Others use the setting sun, and still others, such as pigeons, use Earth's magnetic field to guide them north or south.

While flying at night may not seem like a good idea, it's actually safer. First, there are fewer avian predators hunting for birds at night. Second, night travel allows time during the day to find food in unfamiliar surroundings. Third, wind patterns at night tend to be flat, or laminar. Flat winds don't have the turbulence of daytime winds and can help push the smaller birds along.

# HOW TO USE THIS GUIDE

To help you quickly and easily identify birds, this field guide is organized by color. Refer to the color key on the first page, note the color of the bird, and turn to that section. For example, the Red-headed Woodpecker is black and white with a red head. Because the bird is mostly black-and-white, it will be found in the black-and-white section.

Each color section is also arranged by size, generally with the smaller birds first. Sections may also incorporate the average size in a range, which in some cases reflects size differences between male and female birds. Flip through the pages in the color section to find the bird. If you already know the name of the bird, check the index for the page number.

In some species, the male and female are very different in color. In others, the breeding and winter plumage colors differ. These species will have an inset photograph with a page reference and will be found in two color sections.

You will find a variety of information in the bird description sections. To learn more, turn to the sample on pp. 20–21.

## Range Maps

Range maps are included for each bird. Colored areas indicate where the bird is frequently found. The colors represent the presence of a species during a specific season, not the density, or amount, of birds in the area. Green is used for summer, blue for winter, red for year-round and yellow for migration.

While every effort has been made to depict accurate ranges, these are constantly in flux due to a variety of factors. Changing weather, habitat, species abundance and availability of vital resources, such as food and water, can affect the migration and movement of local populations, causing birds to be found in areas that are atypical for the species. So please use the maps as intended—as general guides only.

female
p. 131

male

# Common Name
## Range Map — *Scientific name* — Color Indicator —

YEAR-ROUND
SUMMER
MIGRATION
WINTER

**Size:** measurement is from head to tip of tail; wingspan may be listed as well

**Male:** brief description of the male bird; may include breeding, winter or other plumages

**Female:** brief description of the female bird, which is sometimes different from the male

**Juvenile:** brief description of the juvenile bird, which often looks like the adult female

**Nest:** kind of nest the bird builds to raise its young; who builds it; number of broods per year

**Eggs:** number of eggs you might expect to see in a nest; color and marking

**Incubation:** average days the parents spend incubating the eggs; who does the incubation

**Fledging:** average days the young spend in the nest after hatching but before they leave the nest; who does the most "childcare" and feeding

**Migration:** type of migrator: complete (seasonal, consistent), partial (seasonal, destination varies), irruptive (unpredictable, depends on the food supply) or non-migrator

**Food:** what the bird eats most of the time (e.g., seeds, insects, fruit, nectar, small mammals, fish) and whether it typically comes to a bird feeder

**Compare:** notes about other birds that look similar and the pages on which they can be found; may include extra information to aid in identification

**Stan's Notes:** Interesting natural history information. This could be something to look or listen for or something to help positively identify the bird. Also includes remarkable features.

female
p. 145

male

YEAR-ROUND

# Eastern Towhee
*Pipilo erythrophthalmus*

**Size:** 7–8" (18–20 cm)

**Male:** Mostly black with rusty-brown sides and a white belly. Long black tail with a white tip. Short, stout, pointed bill and off-white eyes. White wing patches flash in flight.

**Female:** similar to male but brown instead of black

**Juvenile:** light brown, a heavily streaked head, chest and belly, long dark tail with white tip

**Nest:** cup; female builds; 2 broods per year

**Eggs:** 3–4; creamy white with brown markings

**Incubation:** 12–13 days; female incubates

**Fledging:** 10–12 days; male and female feed the young

**Migration:** non-migrator in Florida

**Food:** insects, seeds, fruit; visits ground feeders

**Compare:** American Robin (p. 261) is slightly larger. The Gray Catbird (p. 257) lacks a black "hood" and rusty sides. Common Grackle (p. 31) lacks white belly and has long thin bill.

**Stan's Notes:** Named for its distinctive "tow-hee" call (given by both sexes) but known mostly for its other characteristic call, which sounds like "drink-your-tea!" Will hop backward with both feet (bilateral scratching), raking up leaf litter to locate insects and seeds. The female broods, but male does the most feeding of the young. In southern coastal states, some have red eyes; others have white eyes. The white-eyed variety is found in Florida.

female
p. 147

male

# Brown-headed Cowbird

*Molothrus ater*

YEAR-ROUND

**Size:** 7½" (19 cm)

**Male:** Glossy black with a chocolate-brown head. Dark eyes. Pointed, sharp gray bill.

**Female:** dull brown with a pointed, sharp, gray bill

**Juvenile:** similar to female but with dull-gray plumage and a streaked chest

**Nest:** no nest; lays eggs in nests of other birds

**Eggs:** 5–7; white with brown markings

**Incubation:** 10–13 days; host bird incubates eggs

**Fledging:** 10–11 days; host birds feed the young

**Migration:** non-migrator in Florida

**Food:** insects, seeds; will come to seed feeders

**Compare:** The male Red-winged Blackbird (p. 29) is slightly larger with red-and-yellow patches on upper wings. Common Grackle (p. 31) has a long tail and lacks the brown head. European Starling (p. 27) has a shorter tail.

**Stan's Notes:** Cowbirds are members of the blackbird family. Known as brood parasites, Brown-headed Cowbirds are the only parasitic birds in Florida. Brood parasites lay their eggs in the nests of other birds, leaving the host birds to raise their young. Cowbirds are known to have laid their eggs in the nests of over 200 species of birds. While some birds reject cowbird eggs, most incubate them and raise the young, even to the exclusion of their own. Look for warblers and other birds feeding young birds twice their own size. Named "Cowbird" for its habit of following bison and cattle herds to feed on insects flushed up by the animals.

winter

breeding

# European Starling
## *Sturnus vulgaris*

YEAR-ROUND

| | |
|---|---|
| **Size:** | 7½" (19 cm) |
| **Male:** | Glittering, iridescent purplish black in spring and summer; duller and speckled with white in fall and winter. Long, pointed, yellow bill in spring; gray in fall. Pointed wings. Short tail. |
| **Female:** | same as male |
| **Juvenile:** | similar to adults, with grayish-brown plumage and a streaked chest |
| **Nest:** | cavity; male and female line cavity; 2 broods per year |
| **Eggs:** | 4–6; bluish with brown markings |
| **Incubation:** | 12–14 days; female and male incubate |
| **Fledging:** | 18–20 days; female and male feed the young |
| **Migration:** | non-migrator |
| **Food:** | insects, seeds, fruit; visits seed or suet feeders |
| **Compare:** | The Common Grackle (p. 31) has a long tail. The male Brown-headed Cowbird (p. 25) has a brown head. Look for the shiny, dark feathers to help identify the European Starling. |

**Stan's Notes:** One of our most numerous songbirds. Mimics the songs of up to 20 bird species and imitates sounds, including the human voice. Jaws are more powerful when opening than when closing, enabling the bird to pry open crevices to find insects. Often displaces woodpeckers, chickadees and other cavity-nesting birds. Large families gather with blackbirds in the fall. Not a native bird; 100 starlings were introduced to New York City in 1890–91 from Europe. Bill changes color in spring and fall.

female
p. 159

male

YEAR-ROUND

# Red-winged Blackbird
*Agelaius phoeniceus*

**Size:** 8½" (22 cm)

**Male:** Jet black with red-and-yellow patches (epaulets) on upper wings. Pointed black bill.

**Female:** heavily streaked brown with a pointed brown bill and white eyebrows

**Juvenile:** same as female

**Nest:** cup; female builds; 2–3 broods per year

**Eggs:** 3–4; bluish green with brown markings

**Incubation:** 10–12 days; female incubates

**Fledging:** 11–14 days; female and male feed the young

**Migration:** partial to non-migrator in Florida

**Food:** seeds, insects; visits seed and suet feeders

**Compare:** The male Brown-headed Cowbird (p. 25) is smaller and glossier and has a brown head. The bold red-and-yellow epaulets distinguish the male Red-winged from other blackbirds.

**Stan's Notes:** One of the most widespread and numerous birds in Florida. Found around marshes, wetlands, lakes and rivers. It is a sure sign of spring when these birds return home. Flocks with as many as 10,000 birds have been reported. Males defend their territory by singing from the tops of surrounding vegetation. The male repeats his call from the top of a cattail while showing off his red-and-yellow shoulder patches. The female chooses a mate and often builds her nest over shallow water in a thick stand of cattails. The male can be aggressive when defending the nest. Red-winged Blackbirds feed mostly on seeds in spring and fall, and insects throughout the summer.

# Common Grackle
*Quiscalus quiscula*

YEAR-ROUND

**Size:** 11–13" (28–33 cm)

**Male:** Large, iridescent blackbird with bluish-black head and purplish-brown body. Long black tail. Long, thin bill and bright-golden eyes.

**Female:** similar to male but smaller and duller

**Juvenile:** similar to female

**Nest:** cup; female builds; 2 broods per year

**Eggs:** 4–5; greenish white with brown markings

**Incubation:** 13–14 days; female incubates

**Fledging:** 16–20 days; female and male feed the young

**Migration:** non-migrator to partial in Florida; will move around to find food

**Food:** fruit, seeds, insects; will come to seed and suet feeders

**Compare:** Male Boat-tailed Grackle (p. 37) is larger and has a much longer tail. The European Starling (p. 27) is much smaller with a speckled appearance, and a yellow bill during breeding season. Male Red-winged Blackbird (p. 29) has red-and-yellow wing markings (epaulets).

**Stan's Notes:** Usually nests in small colonies of up to 75 pairs but travels with other blackbird species in large flocks. Known to feed in farm fields. The common name is derived from the Latin word *gracula*, meaning "jackdaw," another species of bird and a term that can refer to any bird in the *Quiscalus* genus. The male holds his tail in a deep V shape during flight. The flight pattern is usually level, as opposed to an undulating movement. Unlike most birds, it has larger muscles for opening its mouth than for closing it, enabling it to pry crevices apart to find hidden insects.

# Common Gallinule
*Gallinula galeata*

**Size:** 13–15" (33–38 cm)

**Male:** Nearly black overall with yellow-tipped red bill. Red forehead. Thin line of white along sides. Yellowish-green legs.

**Female:** same as male

**Juvenile:** same as adult, but brown with white throat and dirty-yellow legs

**Nest:** ground; female and male build; 1–2 broods per year

**Eggs:** 2–10; brown with dark markings

**Incubation:** 19–22 days; female and male incubate

**Fledging:** 40–50 days; female and male feed the young

**Migration:** non-migrator in Florida

**Food:** insects, snails, seeds, green leaves, fruit

**Compare:** American Coot (p. 35) is similar in size but lacks the distinctive yellow-tipped bill and red forehead of Common Gallinule. Purple Gallinule (p. 113) is similar in size but has an iridescent blue-and-green body.

**Stan's Notes:** Also known as Mud Hen or Pond Chicken. A nearly all-black duck-like bird often seen in freshwater marshes and lakes. Walks on floating vegetation or swims while hunting for insects. Females known to lay eggs in other gallinule nests in addition to their own. Builds its nest with cattails and bulrushes and some-times takes an old nest in a low shrub. A cooperative breeder, having young of first brood help raise young of second. Young leave nest usually within a few hours after hatching, but stay with the family for a couple months. Young ride on backs of adults.

# American Coot
*Fulica americana*

**Size:** 13–16" (33–40 cm)

**Male:** Gray-to-black waterbird. Duck-like white bill with a dark band near the tip and a small red patch near the eyes. Small white patch near base of tail. Green legs and feet. Red eyes.

**Female:** same as male

**Juvenile:** much paler than adults, with a gray bill

**Nest:** floating platform; female and male construct; 1 brood per year

**Eggs:** 9–12; pinkish buff with brown markings

**Incubation:** 21–25 days; female and male incubate

**Fledging:** 49–52 days; female and male feed young

**Migration:** non-migrator to complete in Florida

**Food:** insects, aquatic plants

**Compare:** Smaller than most waterfowl, it is the only black, duck-like bird with a white bill.

**Stan's Notes:** Usually seen in large flocks on open water. Not a duck, as it has large lobed toes instead of webbed feet. An excellent diver and swimmer, bobbing its head as it swims. A favorite food of Bald Eagles. It is not often seen in flight, unless it's trying to escape from an eagle. To take off, it scrambles across the surface of the water, flapping its wings. Gives a unique series of creaks, groans and clicks. Anchors its floating platform nest to vegetation. Huge flocks with as many as 1,000 birds gather for migration. Migrates at night. The common name "Coot" comes from the Middle English word *coote*, which was used to describe various waterfowl. Also called Mud Hen.

female
p. 185

male

# Boat-tailed Grackle

*Quiscalus major*

YEAR-ROUND

| | |
|---|---|
| **Size:** | 15–17" (38–43 cm), male<br>13–15" (33–38 cm), female |
| **Male:** | Iridescent blue-black bird. Bright-yellow or dark eyes. Very long keel-shaped tail. |
| **Female:** | brown version of male, lacks iridescence |
| **Juvenile:** | similar to female |
| **Nest:** | cup; female builds; 2 broods per year |
| **Eggs:** | 2–4; pale greenish blue with brown marks |
| **Incubation:** | 13–15 days; female incubates |
| **Fledging:** | 12–15 days; female feeds the young |
| **Migration:** | non-migrator; moves around to find food |
| **Food:** | insects, berries, seeds, fish; visits feeders |
| **Compare:** | Male Common Grackle (p. 31) lacks Boat-tailed's long, distinctive tail. Fish Crow (p. 39) and American Crow (p. 41) are similar but have a very different shape. Look for an iridescent blue head and a very long tail. |

**Stan's Notes:** A noisy bird of coastal saltwater and inland marshes, giving several harsh, high-pitched calls and several squeaks. Eats a wide variety of foods, from grains to fish. Sometimes seen picking insects off the backs of cattle. Will also visit bird feeders. Makes a cup nest with mud or cow dung and grass. Nests in small colonies. Most nesting occurs from February through July and occasionally again from October to December. Boat-taileds north of Gainesville have bright-yellow eyes, but in the rest of the state the birds have dark eyes. More common in Florida than the Common Grackle, although less widespread.

YEAR-ROUND

# Fish Crow
*Corvus ossifragus*

**Size:** 16" (40 cm)

**Male:** All-black bird appearing nearly identical to the American Crow, but with a longer tail and a smaller head and bill.

**Female:** same as male

**Juvenile:** same as adult

**Nest:** platform; female and male construct; 1 brood per year

**Eggs:** 4–5; blue or gray-green with brown marks

**Incubation:** 16–18 days; female and male incubate

**Fledging:** 21–24 days; female and male feed the young

**Migration:** non-migrator

**Food:** insects, carrion, mollusks, berries, seeds

**Compare:** Nearly identical to American Crow (p. 41), but the Fish Crow is smaller, has a longer tail and a smaller head and bill. Fish Crow is most easily differentiated from American Crow by its higher-pitched call.

**Stan's Notes:** Essentially a bird of the coast and along major rivers, but can be found throughout Florida. Not uncommon for it to break open mollusk shells by dropping them onto rocks from above. Very sociable and gregarious. Nests in small colonies, often building a stick nest halfway up a tree. Forms small winter flocks of up to 100 birds, unlike the American Crow, which often forms winter flocks of several thousand. The best way to distinguish between the two crow species is by their remarkably different calls. Fish Crow has a high, nasal "cah."

in flight

YEAR-ROUND

# American Crow
*Corvus brachyrhynchos*

**Size:** 18" (45 cm)

**Male:** All-black bird with black bill, legs and feet. Can have a purple sheen in direct sunlight.

**Female:** same as male

**Juvenile:** same as adult

**Nest:** platform; female builds; 1 brood per year

**Eggs:** 4–6; bluish to olive-green with brown marks

**Incubation:** 18 days; female incubates

**Fledging:** 28–35 days; female and male feed the young

**Migration:** non-migrator to partial migrator

**Food:** fruit, insects, mammals, fish, carrion; will come to seed and suet feeders

**Compare:** Fish Crow (p. 39) is nearly identical, but it is smaller, has a longer tail and a smaller head and bill. American Crow is most easily differentiated from the Fish Crow by its lower-pitched call.

**Stan's Notes:** One of the most recognizable birds in Florida, found in all habitats. Imitates other birds and human voices. One of the smartest of all birds and very social, often entertaining itself by provoking chases with other birds. Eats roadkill but is rarely hit by vehicles. Can live as long as 20 years. Often reuses its nest every year if it's not taken over by a Great Horned Owl. Unmated birds, known as helpers, help to raise the young. Extended families roost together at night, dispersing daily to hunt. Cannot soar on thermals; flaps constantly and glides downward. Gathers in huge communal flocks of up to 10,000 birds in winter.

drying

juvenile

soaring

YEAR-ROUND

# Black Vulture
*Coragyps atratus*

| | |
|---|---|
| **Size:** | 25–28" (63–71 cm); up to 5¼' wingspan |
| **Male:** | Black with dark-gray head and legs. Short tail. In flight, all black with light-gray wing tips. |
| **Female:** | same as male |
| **Juvenile:** | similar to adult |
| **Nest:** | no nest, on a stump or on ground, or takes an abandoned nest; 1 brood per year |
| **Eggs:** | 1–3; light green with dark markings |
| **Incubation:** | 37–45 days; female and male incubate |
| **Fledging:** | 75–80 days; female and male feed the young |
| **Migration:** | non-migrator |
| **Food:** | carrion; occasionally will capture small live mammals |
| **Compare:** | Turkey Vulture (p. 45) is slightly larger, with a bright-red head. Turkey Vulture has two-toned wings with a black leading edge and light-gray trailing edge. The Black Vulture has shorter, gray-tipped wings and a shorter tail. |

**Stan's Notes:** Also called Black Buzzard. A more gregarious bird than the Turkey Vulture. In flight, the Black Vulture holds its wings straight out to its sides unlike the Turkey Vulture, which holds its wings in a V pattern. More aggressive while feeding but less skilled at finding carrion than the Turkey Vulture, it is thought the Black Vulture's sense of smell is less developed. Families stay together up to a year. Often nests and roosts with other Black Vultures. If startled, especially at the nest, it regurgitates with power and accuracy.

soaring

juvenile

drying

YEAR-ROUND

# Turkey Vulture
*Cathartes aura*

**Size:** 26–32" (66–80 cm); up to 6' wingspan

**Male:** Large and black with a naked red head and legs. In flight, wings are two-toned with a black leading edge and a gray trailing edge. Wing tips end in finger-like projections. Tail is long and squared. Ivory bill.

**Female:** same as male but slightly smaller

**Juvenile:** similar to adults, with a gray-to-blackish head and bill

**Nest:** no nest or minimal nest, on a cliff or in a cave, sometimes in a hollow tree; 1 brood per year

**Eggs:** 1–3; white with brown markings

**Incubation:** 38–41 days; female and male incubate

**Fledging:** 66–88 days; female and male feed the young

**Migration:** non-migrator in Florida

**Food:** carrion; parents regurgitate to feed the young

**Compare:** Black Vulture (p. 43) has shorter wings and tail. Bald Eagle (p. 91) is larger and lacks two-toned wings. Look for the obvious naked red head to identify the Turkey Vulture.

**Stan's Notes:** The naked head reduces the risk of feather fouling (picking up diseases) from contact with carcasses. It has a strong bill for tearing apart flesh. Unlike hawks and eagles, it has weak feet more suited for walking than grasping. One of the few birds with a developed sense of smell. Mostly mute, making only grunts and groans. Holds its wings in an upright V shape in flight. Teeters from wing tip to wing tip as it soars and hovers. Seen in trees with wings outstretched, sunning itself and drying after a rain.

YEAR-ROUND

# Muscovy Duck
*Cairina moschata*

**Size:** 28" (71 cm)

**Male:** Wide range of color patterns from a glossy green-black to all white, with some being black and white (pied). Large bumpy patch of flesh, often red, around eyes and base of bill. Usually has a white wing patch, seen when perched and in flight.

**Female:** smaller than male, lacking the bumpy skin patch

**Juvenile:** same as adult but lacks the bumpy skin patch and white wing patch

**Nest:** ground; female builds; 1 brood per year

**Eggs:** 8–20; off-white without markings

**Incubation:** 33–36 days; female incubates

**Fledging:** 60–70 days; female shows young what to eat

**Migration:** non-migrator

**Food:** aquatic insects, grass, seeds

**Compare:** Highly variable-colored duck that is easily identified by the bumpy skin patch around the eyes and base of bill.

**Stan's Notes:** A year-round Florida resident. Naturally occurring in Central and South America, it is a non-native duck that has been released in urban parks, ponds and lakes. Nests at base of trees and in natural cavities. Roosts in trees at night. Not uncommon to nest near human dwellings under shrubbery. Muscovy Ducks can be very aggressive.

in flight

juvenile

crests

drying

# Double-crested Cormorant
*Phalacrocorax auritus*

YEAR-ROUND
MIGRATION

**Size:** 31–35" (79–89 cm); up to 4⅓' wingspan

**Male:** Large black waterbird with unusual blue-teal eyes and a long, snake-like neck. Large gray bill, with yellow at the base and a hooked tip.

**Female:** same as male

**Juvenile:** lighter brown with a grayish chest and neck

**Nest:** platform; male and female construct; 1 brood per year

**Eggs:** 3–4; bluish white without markings

**Incubation:** 25–29 days; female and male incubate

**Fledging:** 37–42 days; male and female feed the young

**Migration:** non-migrator to complete in Florida

**Food:** small fish, aquatic insects

**Compare:** Male Anhinga (p. 51) has white spots and streaks and a long straight bill without a hooked tip. The Turkey Vulture (p. 45) is similar in size and also perches on branches with wings open to dry in sun, but it has a naked red head. American Coot (p. 35) lacks the long neck and long pointed bill.

**Stan's Notes:** Flocks fly in a large V or a line. Usually roosts in large colonies in trees close to water. Swims underwater to catch fish, holding its wings at its sides. This bird's outer feathers soak up water, but its body feathers don't. To dry off, it strikes an upright pose with wings outstretched, facing the sun. Gives grunts, pops and groans. Named "Double-crested" for the crests on its head, which are not often seen. "Cormorant" is a contraction from *corvus marinus*, meaning "crow" or "raven," and "of the sea."

male

female

juvenile

**YEAR-ROUND**

# Anhinga
*Anhinga anhinga*

**Size:** 33–37" (84–94 cm); up to 3¾' wingspan

**Male:** All black with glossy green and white spots and streaks on shoulders and wings. Long neck and tail. Long, narrow yellow bill.

**Female:** similar to male, buff-brown neck and breast

**Juvenile:** similar to female, light-brown-to-white body

**Nest:** platform; female and male build; 1 brood per year

**Eggs:** 2–4; light blue without markings

**Incubation:** 26–29 days; female and male incubate

**Fledging:** 21–25 days; female and male feed the young

**Migration:** non-migrator in Florida

**Food:** fish, aquatic insects, crustaceans and small mammals

**Compare:** The Double-crested Cormorant (p. 49) is slightly smaller and lacks the white spots and streaks of male Anhinga. Cormorant has a shorter bill with a curved tip unlike the long straight bill of the Anhinga.

**Stan's Notes:** Also called Snakebird due to its habit of appearing like a snake—surfacing with just its head and long thin neck showing above the water. It skewers fish, a favorite prey, with its long sharp bill. Unlike ducks and other diving birds, its feathers become waterlogged, which helps it when diving and maneuvering underwater. Afterward, it often strikes a pose with wings spread to dry in the sun (see photo). A strong flier and frequently seen soaring, it is confused with birds of prey. In flight, the long neck and tail help to identify it.

male

female

# Black-and-white Warbler
*Mniotilta varia*

MIGRATION
WINTER

| | |
|---|---|
| **Size:** | 5" (13 cm) |
| **Male:** | Small with zebra-like striping and a black-and-white striped crown. Black cheek patch and chin. White belly. |
| **Female:** | duller than male and lacks a black cheek patch and chin |
| **Juvenile:** | similar to female |
| **Nest:** | cup; female builds; 1 brood per year |
| **Eggs:** | 4–5; white with brown markings |
| **Incubation:** | 10–11 days; female incubates |
| **Fledging:** | 9–12 days; female and male feed the young |
| **Migration:** | complete, to Florida, Mexico, Central America and South America |
| **Food:** | insects |
| **Compare:** | Look for a small black-and-white bird creeping headfirst down trees, like the Brown-headed Nuthatch (p. 229), to identify the Black-and-white Warbler. |

**Stan's Notes:** The only warbler that moves headfirst down a tree trunk. Look for it searching for insect eggs in the bark of large trees. Its song sounds like a slowly turning, squeaky wheel. The female will perform a distraction dance to draw predators away from the nest. Constructs its nest on the ground, concealed beneath dead leaves or at the base of a tree. Fall migrants arrive in August and depart in May. Found in a variety of habitats during winter. Doesn't nest in Florida.

male

female

# Downy Woodpecker
*Dryobates pubescens*

YEAR-ROUND

| | |
|---|---|
| **Size:** | 6" (15 cm) |
| **Male:** | Small woodpecker with a white belly and black-and-white spotted wings. Red mark on the back of the head and a white stripe down the back. Short black bill. |
| **Female:** | same as male but lacks the red mark |
| **Juvenile:** | same as female, some with a red mark near the forehead |
| **Nest:** | cavity with a round entrance hole; male and female excavate; 1 brood per year |
| **Eggs:** | 3–5; white without markings |
| **Incubation:** | 11–12 days; female incubates during the day, male incubates at night |
| **Fledging:** | 20–25 days; male and female feed the young |
| **Migration:** | non-migrator |
| **Food:** | insects, seeds; visits seed and suet feeders |
| **Compare:** | The Hairy Woodpecker (p. 59) is larger. Look for the Downy's shorter, thinner bill. |

**Stan's Notes:** Abundant and widespread where trees are present. This is perhaps the most common woodpecker in the U.S. Stiff tail feathers help to brace it like a tripod as it clings to a tree. Like other woodpeckers, it has a long, barbed tongue to pull insects from tiny places. Mates drum on branches or hollow logs to announce territory, which is rarely larger than 5 acres (2 ha). Repeats a high-pitched "peek-peek" call. Nest cavity is wider at the bottom than at the top and is lined with fallen wood chips. Male performs most of the brooding. During winter, it will roost in a cavity. Undulates in flight.

male

female

WINTER

# Yellow-bellied Sapsucker
*Sphyrapicus varius*

**Size:** 8–9" (20–23 cm)

**Male:** Checkered back with a red forehead, crown and chin. Yellow to tan on the chest and belly. White wing patches are seen flashing in flight.

**Female:** similar to male but with a white chin

**Juvenile:** similar to female, dull brown and lacks any red marking

**Nest:** cavity; female and male excavate, often in a live tree; 1 brood per year

**Eggs:** 5–6; white without markings

**Incubation:** 12–13 days; female incubates during the day, male incubates at night

**Fledging:** 25–29 days; female and male feed the young

**Migration:** complete, to Florida, Mexico and Central America

**Food:** insects, tree sap; comes to suet feeders

**Compare:** The Red-headed Woodpecker (p. 61) has an all-red head. Look for the red chin and crown to identify the male Sapsucker, and the white chin and red crown to identify the female.

**Stan's Notes:** Found in small woods, forests, and suburban and rural areas. Drills rows of holes in trees to bleed the sap. Oozing sap attracts bugs, which it also eats. Defends its sapping sites from other birds that try to drink from the taps. Does not suck sap; rather, it laps the sticky liquid with its long, bristly tongue. A quiet bird, it makes few vocalizations but will meow like a cat. Drums on hollow branches, but unlike other woodpeckers, its rhythm is irregular. Makes short undulating flights with rapid wingbeats.

male

female

# Hairy Woodpecker
*Leuconotopicus villosus*

YEAR-ROUND

**Size:** 9" (23 cm)

**Male:** Black-and-white woodpecker with a white belly. Black wings with rows of white spots. White stripe down the back. Long black bill. Red mark on the back of the head.

**Female:** same as male but lacks the red mark

**Juvenile:** grayer version of the female

**Nest:** cavity with an oval entrance hole; female and male excavate; 1 brood per year

**Eggs:** 3–6; white without markings

**Incubation:** 11–15 days; female incubates during the day, male incubates at night

**Fledging:** 28–30 days; male and female feed the young

**Migration:** non-migrator

**Food:** insects, nuts, seeds; comes to seed and suet feeders

**Compare:** Downy Woodpecker (p. 55) is much smaller and has a much shorter bill. Look for Hairy Woodpecker's long bill, nearly equal to the width of its head.

**Stan's Notes:** A common bird in wooded backyards. Announces its arrival with a sharp chirp before landing on feeders. Responsible for eating many destructive forest insects. Uses its barbed tongue to extract insects from trees. Tiny, bristle-like feathers at the base of the bill protect the nostrils from wood dust. Drums on hollow logs, branches or stovepipes in spring to announce territory. Prefers to excavate nest cavities in live trees. Excavates a larger, more-oval-shaped entrance than the round entrance hole of the Downy Woodpecker. Makes short flights from tree to tree.

juvenile

YEAR-ROUND

# Red-headed Woodpecker
*Melanerpes erythrocephalus*

**Size:** 9" (23 cm)

**Male:** All-red head with a solid black back. White chest, belly and rump. Black wings with large white wing patches seen flashing in flight. Black tail. Gray legs and bill.

**Female:** same as male

**Juvenile:** gray brown with white chest, lacks any red

**Nest:** cavity; male builds with help from female; 1 brood per year

**Eggs:** 4–5; white without markings

**Incubation:** 12–13 days; female and male incubate

**Fledging:** 27–30 days; female and male feed the young

**Migration:** partial migrator; will move to areas with an abundant supply of nuts

**Food:** insects, nuts, fruit; visits suet and seed feeders

**Compare:** No other woodpecker in Florida has an all-red head. The Pileated Woodpecker (p. 79) is the only other woodpecker with a solid black back, but it has a partially red head.

**Stan's Notes:** One of the few non-dimorphic woodpeckers, with males and females that look alike. Bill is strong enough to excavate a nest cavity only in soft, dead trees. Prefers open woodlands or woodland edges with many dead or rotting branches. Nests later than its close relative, the Red-bellied Woodpecker, and will often take its cavity, if vacant. Unlike other woodpeckers, which use nest cavities just once briefly, it may use the same cavity for several years in a row. Often perches on top of dead snags. Stores acorns and other nuts. Gives a shrill, hoarse "churr" call.

male

female

YEAR-ROUND

# Red-bellied Woodpecker
*Melanerpes carolinus*

**Size:** 9–9½" (23–24 cm)

**Male:** Black-and-white "zebra-backed" woodpecker with a white rump. Red crown extends down the nape of the neck. Tan chest. Pale-red tinge on the belly, often hard to see.

**Female:** same as male but with a light-gray crown and a red nape

**Juvenile:** gray version of adults; lacks a red crown and red nape

**Nest:** cavity; female and male excavate; 1 brood per year

**Eggs:** 4–5; white without markings

**Incubation:** 12–14 days; female incubates during the day, male incubates at night

**Fledging:** 24–27 days; female and male feed the young

**Migration:** non-migrator; moves around to find food

**Food:** insects, nuts, fruit; visits suet and seed feeders

**Compare:** Similar to the Northern Flicker (p. 177) and Yellow-bellied Sapsucker (p. 57). Look for the zebra-striped back to help identify the Red-bellied Woodpecker.

**Stan's Notes:** Likes shady woodlands, forest edges and backyards. Digs holes in rotten wood to find spiders, centipedes, beetles and more. Hammers acorns and berries into crevices of trees for winter food. Returns to the same tree to excavate a new nest below that of the previous year. Undulating flight with rapid wingbeats. Gives a loud "querrr" call and a low "chug-chug-chug." Named for the pale red tinge on its belly. Often kicked out of nest hole by European Starlings. Expanding its range all over the country.

breeding

winter

# Ruddy Turnstone
*Arenaria interpres*

**Size:** 9½" (24 cm)

**Male:** Breeding male has a white breast and belly with a black bib. Wings and back are black and chestnut. Head has a black-and-white marking. Orange legs. Slightly upturned black bill. Winter male has a brown-and-white head and breast pattern.

**Female:** similar to male but duller

**Juvenile:** similar to adults, but black-and-white head has a scaly appearance

**Nest:** ground; female builds; 1 brood per year

**Eggs:** 3–4; olive-green with dark markings

**Incubation:** 22–24 days; male and female incubate

**Fledging:** 19–21 days; male feeds the young

**Migration:** complete, to coastal Florida, South America

**Food:** aquatic insects, fish, mollusks, crustaceans, worms, eggs

**Compare:** Unusually ornamented shorebird. Look for the striking black-and-white pattern on the head and neck, and orange legs to identify.

**Stan's Notes:** A common migrant and winter resident. Also known as Rock Plover. Named "Turnstone" because it turns stones over on rocky beaches to find food. Known for its unusual behavior of robbing and eating other birds' eggs. Hangs around crabbing operations to eat scraps from nets. Can be very tolerant of humans when feeding. Females often leave before their young leave the nest (fledge), resulting in males raising the young. Males have a bare spot on the belly (brood patch) to warm the young, something only females normally have.

breeding

winter
p. 269

# Black-bellied Plover
*Pluvialis squatarola*

MIGRATION
WINTER

| | |
|---|---|
| **Size:** | 11–12" (28–30 cm) |
| **Male:** | Striking black and white breeding plumage. Belly, breast, sides, face and neck are black. Cap, nape of neck, and belly near tail are white. Black legs and bill. |
| **Female:** | less black on belly and breast than male |
| **Juvenile:** | grayer than adults, with much less black |
| **Nest:** | ground; male and female construct; 1 brood per year |
| **Eggs:** | 3–4; pinkish or greenish with black-brown markings |
| **Incubation:** | 26–27 days; male incubates during the day, female incubates at night |
| **Fledging:** | 35–45 days; male feeds the young, the young learn quickly to feed themselves |
| **Migration:** | complete, to coastal Florida |
| **Food:** | insects |
| **Compare:** | Breeding Dunlin (p. 155) is slightly smaller, with a rusty back and long down-curved bill. Look for Black-bellied's large black patch on the belly, face and chest, and a white cap. |

**Stan's Notes:** Males perform a "butterfly" courtship flight to attract females. Female leaves male and young about 12 days after the eggs hatch. Breeds at age 3. A winter resident along the Florida coast. Begins arriving in July and August (fall migration). During flight, in any plumage, displays a white rump and stripe on wings with black axillaries (armpits). Often darts across the ground to grab an insect and run. Can be very common on the beach during winter.

# Black-necked Stilt

*Himantopus mexicanus*

YEAR-ROUND
SUMMER

| | |
|---|---|
| **Size:** | 14" (36 cm) |
| **Male:** | Black-and-white with ridiculously long red-to-pink legs. Upper parts of the head, neck and back are black. Lower parts are white. Long black bill. |
| **Female:** | similar to male but browner on back |
| **Juvenile:** | similar to female but brown instead of black |
| **Nest:** | ground; female and male construct; 1 brood per year |
| **Eggs:** | 3–5; off-white with dark markings |
| **Incubation:** | 22–26 days; male incubates during the day, female incubates at night |
| **Fledging:** | 28–32 days; female and male feed the young |
| **Migration:** | complete to non-migrator in Florida |
| **Food:** | aquatic insects |
| **Compare:** | Outrageous length of the red-to-pink legs makes this shorebird hard to confuse with any other. |

**Stan's Notes:** Although a year-round resident in southern Florida, it can be found along the East Coast and as far north as the Great Lakes. Nests alone or in small colonies in open areas. This very vocal bird of shallow marshes gives a "kek-kek-kek" call. Its legs are up to 10 inches (25 cm) long and may be the longest legs in the bird world in proportion to the body. Known to transport water with water-soaked belly feathers (belly-soaking) to cool eggs in hot weather. Aggressively defends its nest, eggs and young. Young leave the nest shortly after hatching.

female
p. 193

male

WINTER

# Hooded Merganser
*Lophodytes cucullatus*

**Size:** 16–19" (40–48 cm)

**Male:** Black and white with rust-brown sides. Crest "hood" raises to show a large white patch on each side of the head. Long, thin, black bill.

**Female:** brown and rust with ragged, rust-red "hair" and a long, thin, brown bill

**Juvenile:** similar to female

**Nest:** cavity; female lines an old woodpecker cavity or a nest box near water; 1 brood per year

**Eggs:** 10–12; white without markings

**Incubation:** 32–33 days; female incubates

**Fledging:** 71 days; female feeds the young

**Migration:** complete, to Florida

**Food:** small fish, aquatic insects, crustaceans (especially crayfish)

**Compare:** The male Wood Duck (p. 301) has a green head. The white patch on the head and rust-brown sides distinguish the male Hoodie.

**Stan's Notes:** A small diving bird of shallow ponds, sloughs, lakes and rivers, usually in small groups. Quick, low flight across the water, with fast wingbeats. Male has a deep, rolling call. Female gives a hoarse quack. Nests in wooded areas. Female will lay some eggs in the nests of other Hooded Mergansers or Wood Ducks, resulting in 20–25 eggs in some nests. Rarely, she shares a nest, sitting with a Wood Duck.

female
p. 195

male

WINTER

# Ring-necked Duck
*Aythya collaris*

**Size:** 16–19" (41–48 cm)

**Male:** Striking black duck with light-gray-to-white sides. Blue bill with a bold white ring and a thinner ring at the base. Peaked head with a sloped forehead.

**Female:** brown with darker-brown back and crown, light-brown sides, gray face, white eye-ring, white ring around the bill, and peaked head

**Juvenile:** similar to female

**Nest:** ground; female builds; 1 brood per year

**Eggs:** 8–10; olive-gray to brown without markings

**Incubation:** 26–27 days; female incubates

**Fledging:** 49–56 days; female teaches the young to feed

**Migration:** complete, to Florida, other southern states

**Food:** aquatic plants and insects

**Compare:** Look for the blue bill with a bold white ring to identify the male Ring-necked Duck.

**Stan's Notes:** One of the most abundant wintering ducks in the state. Usually in larger freshwater lakes rather than saltwater marshes, in small flocks or just pairs. Watch for this diving duck to dive underwater to forage for food. Springs up off the water to take flight. Flattens its crown when diving. Male gives a quick series of grating barks and grunts. Female gives high-pitched peeps. Named "Ring-necked" for its cinnamon collar, which is nearly impossible to see in the field. Also called Ring-billed Duck due to the white ring on its bill.

skimming

# Black Skimmer
*Rynchops niger*

YEAR-ROUND
MIGRATION
WINTER

**Size:** 18" (45 cm); up to 3½' wingspan

**Male:** A striking black-and-white bird with black on top and white on bottom. Very distinct black-tipped red bill with lower bill longer than the upper. Red legs tuck up and out of sight when in flight.

**Female:** similar to male but smaller

**Juvenile:** similar to adults, spotty brown on top

**Nest:** ground; female and male construct; 1 brood per year

**Eggs:** 3–5; bluish white with brown markings

**Incubation:** 21–23 days; female and male incubate

**Fledging:** 23–25 days; female and male feed the young

**Migration:** non-migrator to complete in Florida

**Food:** small fish, shrimp

**Compare:** Royal Tern (p. 335) has a similar shape, but it lacks the black back and black-tipped red bill. Look for a large black-and-white bird, with a lower bill longer than the upper bill, that skims across the water.

**Stan's Notes:** Also called Scissorbill or Razorbill, referring to this bird's unusual long bill. Uses its unique bill while in flight to cut through the water to catch fish or shrimp close to the surface. Commonly feeds with several other skimmers. Often seen flying to and from nesting colony with fish in its bill. Nests in large colonies, often associated with terns. Found along the East and Gulf Coasts.

in flight

# American Oystercatcher
*Haematopus palliatus*

YEAR-ROUND

| | |
|---|---|
| **Size:** | 18–19" (45–48 cm) |
| **Male:** | Large shorebird with dark-brown sides, wings and back, and a white chest and belly. Black head. Red ring around the eyes and a large red-orange bill. Pink legs. |
| **Female:** | same as male |
| **Juvenile:** | more gray than black and lacks the brightly colored bill |
| **Nest:** | ground; male and female construct; 1 brood per year |
| **Eggs:** | 2–4; olive with sparse brown markings |
| **Incubation:** | 24–29 days; female incubates during the day, male incubates at night |
| **Fledging:** | 35–40 days; male and female feed the young, the young learn quickly to feed themselves |
| **Migration:** | non-migrator to partial along coastal Florida |
| **Food:** | shellfish, insects, aquatic insects, worms |
| **Compare:** | Breeding Black-bellied Plover (p. 67) is smaller. Look for the Oystercatcher's large and obvious red-orange bill. |

**Stan's Notes:** A large, stunningly beautiful bird that stands out on the beach. This chunky shorebird has a flattened, heavy bill, which it uses to pry open shellfish and probe sand for insects and worms. Oystercatchers open oysters in two different ways. Some, known as "stabbers" sneak up on mollusks and stab their bills between shells before they have a chance to close. Others, called "hammerers" shatter one half.

male

female

# Pileated Woodpecker
*Dryocopus pileatus*

**Size:** 19" (48 cm)

**Male:** Crow-size woodpecker with a black back and bright-red forehead, crest and mustache. Long gray bill. White leading edge of wings flashes brightly during flight.

**Female:** same as male but with a black forehead; lacks a red mustache

**Juvenile:** similar to adults but duller and browner

**Nest:** cavity; male and female excavate; 1 brood per year

**Eggs:** 3–5; white without markings

**Incubation:** 15–18 days; female incubates during the day, male incubates at night

**Fledging:** 26–28 days; female and male feed the young

**Migration:** non-migrator; moves around to find food

**Food:** insects; will come to suet and peanut feeders

**Compare:** The Red-headed Woodpecker (p. 61) is about half the size and has an all-red head. Look for the bright-red crest and exceptionally large size to identify the Pileated Woodpecker.

**Stan's Notes:** Our largest woodpecker. The common name comes from the Latin *pileatus*, which means "wearing a cap." A relatively shy bird that prefers large tracts of woodland. Drums on hollow branches, chimneys and so forth to announce its territory. Excavates oval holes up to several feet long in tree trunks, looking for insects to eat. Large wood chips lie on the ground by excavated trees. Favorite food is carpenter ants. Feeds regurgitated insects to its young. Young emerge from the nest looking just like the adults.

soaring

**YEAR-ROUND**

# Osprey
*Pandion haliaetus*

| | |
|---|---|
| **Size:** | 21–24" (53–61 cm); up to 5½' wingspan |
| **Male:** | Large eagle-like bird with a white chest, belly and head. Dark eye line. Nearly black back. Black "wrist" marks on the wings. Dark bill. |
| **Female:** | same as male but slightly larger and with a necklace of brown streaks |
| **Juvenile:** | similar to adults, with a light-tan breast |
| **Nest:** | platform on a raised wooden platform, man-made tower or tall dead tree; female and male build; 1 brood per year |
| **Eggs:** | 2–4; white with brown markings |
| **Incubation:** | 32–42 days; female and male incubate |
| **Fledging:** | 48–58 days; male and female feed the young |
| **Migration:** | non-migrator to partial in Florida |
| **Food:** | fish |
| **Compare:** | The juvenile Bald Eagle (p. 91) is brown with white speckles. The adult Bald Eagle has an all-white head and tail. Look for the white belly and dark eye line to identify the Osprey. |

**Stan's Notes:** The only species in its family, and the only raptor that plunges into water feetfirst to catch fish. Always near water. Can hover for a few seconds before diving. Carries fish in a head-first position for better aerodynamics. Wings angle back in flight. Often harassed by Bald Eagles for its catch. Gives a high-pitched, whistle-like call, often calling in flight as a warning. Mates have a long-term pair bond. May not migrate to the same wintering grounds. Was nearly extinct but is now doing well.

soaring

juvenile

# Crested Caracara
*Caracara cheriway*

YEAR-ROUND

**Size:** 22–25" (56–63 cm); up to 4¼' wingspan

**Male:** Black body and wings with a white chin, upper neck and wing tips. Large, obvious black crest. A long neck. Orange facial skin just behind a large gray bill. Long, strong yellow legs. White tail with a black terminal band, seen in flight.

**Female:** same as male, but slightly larger

**Juvenile:** similar to adult, but black areas are brown, and white areas are tan

**Nest:** platform; female builds; 1 brood per year

**Eggs:** 2–3; white or pinkish with brown markings

**Incubation:** 26–30 days; female and male incubate

**Fledging:** 40–60 days; female and male feed young

**Migration:** non-migrator; moves around to find food

**Food:** carrion, small mammals, insects, reptiles

**Compare:** Osprey (p. 81) is similar in size, but lacks the black belly and orange facial skin. Look for a bold black-and-white pattern and long yellow legs to help identify.

**Stan's Notes:** Largest member of the falcon family. Found in open savanna or tropical scrubland habitat, often near ranches. Feeds mainly on roadkill, often coursing (patrolling) at low elevations on roads at sunrise. Very different from all other raptors in North America, using its legs to stalk and chase prey such as mice. Often seen with vultures, and often in pairs. Glides on flat wings, unlike vultures in flight, which hold their wings upward in a semi-V shape. Roosts in trees at night. Facial skin can change color, usually to pale gray.

in flight

juvenile

# Black-crowned Night-Heron
*Nycticorax nycticorax*

YEAR-ROUND
MIGRATION

**Size:** 22–27" (56–69 cm); up to 3½' wingspan

**Male:** A stocky, hunched and inactive heron with black back and crown, white belly and gray wings. Long dark bill and bright-red eyes. Short dull-yellow legs. Breeding adult has 2 long white plumes on crown.

**Female:** same as male

**Juvenile:** golden-brown head and back with white spots, streaked breast, yellow-orange eyes, brown bill

**Nest:** platform; female and male build; 1 brood per year

**Eggs:** 3–5; light blue without markings

**Incubation:** 24–26 days; female and male incubate

**Fledging:** 42–48 days; female and male feed the young

**Migration:** partial to non-migrator in Florida

**Food:** fish, aquatic insects

**Compare:** Yellow-crowned Night-Heron (p. 287) is similar in size, but has a white cheek patch and lacks the Black-crowned's black back. A perching Great Blue Heron (p. 291) looks twice the size of a Black-crowned. Look for a short-necked heron with a black back and crown.

**Stan's Notes:** A very secretive bird, this heron is most active near dawn and dusk (crepuscular). It hunts alone, but it nests in small colonies. Roosts in trees during the day. Often squawks if disturbed from the daytime roost. Often seen being harassed by other herons during the day. Stalks quiet backwaters in search of small fish and crabs.

in flight

# Swallow-tailed Kite
*Elanoides forficatus*

SUMMER

**Size:** 23" (58 cm); up to 4¼' wingspan

**Male:** A white head, chest and belly. Black back, wings and tail. In flight, white leading edge of narrow pointed wings, a black trailing edge and a long, deeply forked tail. In the right light, black back and wings appear metallic green-blue.

**Female:** same as male

**Juvenile:** same as adult, but has a shorter tail

**Nest:** platform; female and male build; 1 brood per year

**Eggs:** 2–4; white with dark markings

**Incubation:** 26–28 days; female and male incubate

**Fledging:** 36–42 days; female and male feed young

**Migration:** complete, to Central and South America

**Food:** insects, snakes, lizards, frogs, mammals

**Compare:** Osprey (p. 81) is slightly larger and shares its black-and-white pattern. Look for Swallow-tailed Kite's deeply forked tail, which is found on no other bird of prey in Florida.

**Stan's Notes:** Stunning in flight, the contrasting colors and forked tail easily identify it. Feeds while in flight. Also drinks on the wing, skimming across the surface of water like a swallow. Soars with its wings flat. Rarely hovers like other birds of prey. A very agile flier, it will collect sticks for the nest as Ospreys do, breaking off sticks with its feet as it flies. Semi-social, a couple of birds will share the same territory. Prefers open woods and river bottoms. Found mostly in Florida. Its range was once as far north as Minnesota.

breeding

winter

# Common Loon
*Gavia immer*

**MIGRATION WINTER**

**Size:** 28–36" (71–91 cm)

**Male:** Checkerboard back, black head, white neck-lace. Deep-red eyes. Long, pointed black bill. Winter plumage has a gray body and bill.

**Female:** same as male

**Juvenile:** similar to winter plumage, but lacks red eyes

**Nest:** ground, usually at the shoreline; female and male build; 1 brood per year

**Eggs:** 2; olive-brown, occasionally brown markings

**Incubation:** 26–31 days; female and male incubate

**Fledging:** 75–80 days; female and male feed the young

**Migration:** complete, to coastal Florida, other southern coastal states and Mexico

**Food:** fish, aquatic insects, crayfish, salamanders

**Compare:** The Double-crested Cormorant (p. 49) has a black chest and gray bill with a hooked tip and yellow at the base. Look for a checker-board back to identify the Common Loon.

**Stan's Notes:** Hunts for fish by eyesight and prefers clear, clean lakes. A great swimmer, but its legs are set so far back that it has a hard time walking. "Loon" comes from the Scandinavian term *lom*, meaning "lame," for the awkward way it walks on land. To take off, it faces into the wind and runs on the water while flapping. Its wailing call suggests wild laughter, which led to the phrase "crazy as a loon." Also gives soft hoots. In the water, young ride on the backs of their parents for about 10 days. Adults perform distraction displays to protect the young. Very sensitive to disturbance during nesting and will abandon the nest.

soaring

juvenile

soaring
juvenile

# Bald Eagle
*Haliaeetus leucocephalus*

YEAR-ROUND
WINTER

**Size:** 31–37" (79–94 cm); up to 7½' wingspan

**Male:** White head and tail contrast sharply with the dark-brown-to-black body and wings. Large, curved yellow bill and yellow feet.

**Female:** same as male but larger

**Juvenile:** dark brown with white speckles and spots on the body and wings; gray bill

**Nest:** massive platform, usually in a tree; female and male build; 1 brood per year

**Eggs:** 2–3; off-white without markings

**Incubation:** 34–36 days; female and male incubate

**Fledging:** 75–90 days; female and male feed the young

**Migration:** non-migrator to partial migrator

**Food:** fish, carrion, birds (mainly ducks)

**Compare:** Black Vulture (p. 43) is smaller, has a shorter tail and lacks the adult Bald Eagle's white head and tail. Turkey Vulture (p. 45) is smaller and flies with its two-toned wings held in a V shape, unlike the straight-out wing position of the Bald Eagle.

**Stan's Notes:** Nearly became extinct due to DDT poisoning and illegal killing. Returns to the same nest each year, adding more sticks and enlarging it to huge proportions, at times up to 1,000 pounds (450 kg). In their midair mating ritual, one eagle flips upside down and locks talons with another. Both tumble, then break apart to continue flight. Not uncommon for juveniles to perform this mating ritual even though they have not reached breeding age. Long-term pair bond but will switch mates when not successful at reproducing. Juveniles attain the white head and tail at 4–5 years of age.

in flight

# Wood Stork
*Mycteria americana*

YEAR-ROUND
SUMMER

**Size:** 42–44" (107–112 cm); up to 5' wingspan

**Male:** An all-white body with a bald, nearly black head. Tail, wing tips and entire trailing edge of wings are black, as seen in flight. Black legs and pink feet. Thick, slightly down-curved dark bill.

**Female:** same as male

**Juvenile:** similar to adult but with a gray-to-brown head and neck and a dull-yellow bill

**Nest:** platform; female and male build; 1 brood per year

**Eggs:** 2–4; white without markings

**Incubation:** 28–32 days; male and female incubate

**Fledging:** 55–60 days; female and male feed the young

**Migration:** non-migrator to partial in Florida

**Food:** fish, amphibians, aquatic insects, snails

**Compare:** Great Egret (p. 345) is similarly sized but lacks Wood Stork's dark head and down-curved bill. Snowy Egret (p. 339) is about half the size of Wood Stork. Look for Wood Stork's black tail, wing tips and edge of wings in flight.

**Stan's Notes:** On state and federal threatened species lists. Like many wading birds, its population has declined; its numbers are about 40 percent of a century ago. Feeds by swinging its open bill through water until it contacts prey, then snaps bill shut. Shuffles its feet to stir up fish before capturing. Nests in large colonies, often high up in trees. Usually doesn't breed until it reaches 4–5 years of age. Abandons eggs or young when food supply is short.

# Blue-gray Gnatcatcher
*Polioptila caerulea*

**Size:** 4" (10 cm)

**Male:** A light-blue-to-gray head, back, breast and wings, with a white belly. Black forehead and eyebrows. Prominent white eye-ring. Long black tail with a white undertail, often held cocked above the rest of body.

**Female:** same as male but grayer and lacking black on the head

**Juvenile:** similar to female

**Nest:** cup; female and male construct; 1 brood per year

**Eggs:** 4–5; pale blue with dark markings

**Incubation:** 10–13 days; female and male incubate

**Fledging:** 10–12 days; female and male feed the young

**Migration:** non-migrator to partial in Florida

**Food:** insects

**Compare:** The only small blue bird with a black tail. Very active near the nest, look for it flitting around upper branches in search of insects.

**Stan's Notes:** Seen throughout the state in a wide variety of forest types. Listen for its wheezy call notes to help locate it. A fun and easy bird to watch. Flicks its tail up and down and from side to side while calling. In many years, it nests so early that by mid-June it is no longer defending territory. Like many open-woodland nesters, it is a common cowbird host. Although the population is abundant and widespread, it has been decreasing in the recent past. Many northern Blue-gray Gnatcatchers winter in Florida.

female
p. 131

male

SUMMER
MIGRATION
WINTER

# Indigo Bunting
*Passerina cyanea*

**Size:** 5½" (14 cm)

**Male:** Vibrant-blue finch-like bird. Dark markings scattered on wings and tail.

**Female:** light-brown with faint markings

**Juvenile:** similar to female

**Nest:** cup; female builds; 2 broods per year

**Eggs:** 3–4; pale blue without markings

**Incubation:** 12–13 days; female incubates

**Fledging:** 10–11 days; female feeds the young

**Migration:** complete, to southern Florida, Mexico, Central America and South America

**Food:** insects, seeds, fruit; will visit seed feeders

**Compare:** The male Eastern Bluebird (p. 103) is larger and has a rust-red chest. Look for the bright-blue plumage to identify the male Indigo Bunting.

**Stan's Notes:** Seen along woodland edges and in parks and yards, feeding on insects. Comes to seed feeders early in spring, before insects are plentiful. Usually only the males are noticed. The male often sings from treetops to attract a mate. The female is quiet. Actually a gray bird, without blue pigment in its feathers: like Blue Jays and other blue birds, sunlight is refracted within the structure of the feathers, making them appear blue. Plumage is iridescent in direct sun, duller in shade. Molts in spring to acquire body feathers with gray tips, which quickly wear off, revealing the bright-blue plumage. Molts in fall and appears like the female during winter. Migrates at night in flocks of 5–10 birds. Males return before the females and juveniles, often to the nest site of the preceding year. Juveniles move to within a mile of their birth site.

# Tree Swallow
*Tachycineta bicolor*

YEAR-ROUND
MIGRATION

**Size:** 5–6" (13–15 cm)

**Male:** Blue-green in spring, greener in fall. Changes color in direct sunlight. White from chin to belly. Long, pointed wing tips. Notched tail.

**Female:** similar to male but duller

**Juvenile:** gray brown with a white belly and a grayish breast band

**Nest:** cavity; female and male line a vacant woodpecker cavity or nest box; 2 broods per year

**Eggs:** 4–6; white without markings

**Incubation:** 13–16 days; female incubates

**Fledging:** 20–24 days; female and male feed the young

**Migration:** non-migrator to partial in Florida

**Food:** insects

**Compare:** The Purple Martin (p. 105) is much larger and darker. The Barn Swallow (p. 101) has a rusty belly and a long, deeply forked tail. Look for the white chin, chest and belly and the notched tail to help identify the Tree Swallow.

**Stan's Notes:** Most common at coastal beaches, freshwater ponds, lakes and agricultural fields. Can be attracted to your yard with a nest box. Competes with Eastern Bluebirds for cavities and nest boxes. Builds a grass nest within and will travel long distances, looking for dropped feathers for the lining. Watch for it playing and chasing after feathers. Flies with rapid wingbeats, then glides. Gives a series of gurgles and chirps. Chatters when upset or threatened. Eats many nuisance bugs. A year-round resident in Florida, gathering in large flocks during migration and winter.

SUMMER
MIGRATION

# Barn Swallow
*Hirundo rustica*

**Size:** 7" (18 cm)

**Male:** Sleek swallow. Blue-black back, cinnamon belly and reddish-brown chin. White spots on a long, deeply forked tail.

**Female:** same as male but with a whitish belly

**Juvenile:** similar to adults, with a tan belly and chin, and shorter tail

**Nest:** cup; female and male build; 2 broods per year

**Eggs:** 4–5; white with brown markings

**Incubation:** 13–17 days; female incubates

**Fledging:** 18–23 days; female and male feed the young

**Migration:** complete, to South America

**Food:** insects (prefers beetles, wasps, flies)

**Compare:** The Tree Swallow (p. 99) is white from chin to belly. The Purple Martin (p. 105) is larger and has a dark-purple belly. The Chimney Swift (p. 121) has a narrow, pointed tail. Look for the deeply forked tail to identify the Barn Swallow.

**Stan's Notes:** Seen in wetlands, farms, suburban yards and parks. Of the eight swallow species in Florida, this is the only one with a deeply forked tail. Unlike other swallows, it rarely glides in flight. Usually flies low over land or water. Drinks as it flies, skimming water, or will sip water droplets on wet leaves. Bathes while flying through rain or sprinklers. Gives a twittering warble, followed by a mechanical sound. Builds a mud nest with up to 1,000 beak-loads of mud. Nests on barns and houses, under bridges and in other sheltered places. Often nests in colonies of 4–6 birds; sometimes nests alone.

male

female

# Eastern Bluebird
*Sialia sialis*

YEAR-ROUND

| | |
|---|---|
| **Size:** | 7" (18 cm) |
| **Male:** | Sky-blue head, back and tail. Rust-red breast and white belly. |
| **Female:** | grayer than male, with a faint rusty breast and faint blue wings and tail |
| **Juvenile:** | similar to female but with spots on the breast and blue wing markings |
| **Nest:** | cavity, vacant woodpecker cavity or nest box; female adds a soft lining; 2 broods per year |
| **Eggs:** | 4–5; pale blue without markings |
| **Incubation:** | 12–14 days; female incubates |
| **Fledging:** | 15–18 days; male and female feed the young |
| **Migration:** | non-migrator in most of Florida |
| **Food:** | insects, fruit; comes to shallow dishes with live or dead mealworms, and to suet feeders |
| **Compare:** | The male Indigo Bunting (p. 97) is nearly all blue. The Blue Jay (p. 109) is much larger and has a crest. Look for the rusty breast to help identify the Eastern Bluebird. |

**Stan's Notes:** Once nearly eliminated from Florida due to a lack of nest cavities. Thanks to people who installed thousands of nest boxes, bluebirds now thrive. Prefers open habitats, such as farm fields, pastures and roadsides, but also likes forest edges, parks and yards. Often perches on trees or fence posts and drops to the ground to grab bugs, especially grasshoppers. Makes short flights from tree to tree. Song is a distinctive "churlee chur chur-lee." A year-round resident that is joined by many northern migrants, swelling populations during winter. The rust-red breast is like that of the American Robin, its cousin.

male

female

SUMMER

# Purple Martin
*Progne subis*

**Size:** 8½" (22 cm)

**Male:** Iridescent with a purple-to-black head, back and belly. Black wings and a notched black tail.

**Female:** grayish-purple head and back, darker wings and tail, whitish belly

**Juvenile:** same as female

**Nest:** cavity; female and male line the cavity of the house; 1 brood per year

**Eggs:** 4–5; white without markings

**Incubation:** 15–18 days; female incubates

**Fledging:** 26–30 days; male and female feed the young

**Migration:** complete, to South America

**Food:** insects

**Compare:** Usually seen only in groups. The male Purple Martin is the only swallow with a very dark-purplish belly.

**Stan's Notes:** The largest swallow species in North America. Once nested in tree cavities; now nests almost exclusively in man-made, apartment-style houses. The most successful colonies often nest in multiunit nest boxes within 100 feet (30 m) of a human dwelling near a lake. Main diet consists of dragonflies, not mosquitoes, as once thought. Gives a continuous stream of chirps, creaks and rattles, along with a shout-like "churrr" and chortle. Often drinks in flight, skimming water, and bathes in flight, flying through rain. Returns to the same nest site each year; the males arrive before the females and yearlings. The young leave to form new colonies. Large colonies gather in fall before migrating to South America.

YEAR-ROUND

# Florida Scrub-Jay
*Aphelocoma coerulescens*

**Size:** 11" (28 cm)

**Male:** A dark-blue body with a lighter-blue head. Dirty-white belly and a white forehead. A proportionately long tail.

**Female:** same as male

**Juvenile:** same as adult

**Nest:** cup; female and male construct; 1 brood per year

**Eggs:** 3–6; pale green with dark markings

**Incubation:** 15–17 days; female incubates

**Fledging:** 18–20 days; female and male feed young

**Migration:** non-migrator

**Food:** insects, fruit, seeds

**Compare:** The "other" jay in Florida. Darker blue than Blue Jay (p. 109) and lacks Blue Jay's crest and black necklace. Look for the Scrub-Jay's white forehead and long tail to identify it.

**Stan's Notes:** Found in central Florida and nowhere else, the Scrub-Jay is well known for its cooperative breeding system in which the young from one year help to raise the young of the new year. Has a wide variety of raspy, hoarse calls. Prefers a transitional scrubby habitat, usually of oak trees around 10 feet (3 m) tall with some openings. Not a backyard bird, like the Blue Jay. A threatened species, its population has declined up to 90 percent over the last century due to habitat loss.

YEAR-ROUND

# Blue Jay
*Cyanocitta cristata*

**Size:** 12" (30 cm)

**Male:** Bright light-blue-and-white bird with a black necklace and gray belly. Large crest moves up and down at will. White face, wing bars and tip of tail. Black tail bands.

**Female:** same as male

**Juvenile:** same as adult but duller

**Nest:** cup; female and male construct; 1–2 broods per year

**Eggs:** 4–5; green to blue with brown markings

**Incubation:** 16–18 days; female incubates

**Fledging:** 17–21 days; female and male feed the young

**Migration:** non-migrator to partial migrator; will move around to find an abundant food source

**Food:** insects, fruit, carrion, seeds, nuts; visits seed feeders, ground feeders with corn or peanuts

**Compare:** The Belted Kingfisher (p. 111) has a larger, more ragged crest. The Eastern Bluebird (p. 103) is much smaller and has a rust-red breast. Look for the large crest to help identify the Blue Jay.

**Stan's Notes:** Highly intelligent, solving problems, gathering food and communicating more than other birds. Loud and noisy; mimics other birds. Known as the alarm of the forest, screaming at intruders. Imitates hawk calls around feeders to scare off other birds. One of the few birds to cache food; can remember where it hid thousands of nuts. Carries food in a pouch under its tongue (sublingually). Eats eggs and young from other nests. Feathers lack blue pigment; refracted sunlight causes the blue appearance.

male

female

YEAR-ROUND
WINTER

# Belted Kingfisher
*Megaceryle alcyon*

**Size:** 12–14" (30–36 cm)

**Male:** Blue with white belly, blue-gray chest band, and black wing tips. Ragged crest moves up and down at will. Large head. Long, thick, black bill. White spot by eyes. Red-brown eyes.

**Female:** same as male but with rusty flanks and a rusty chest band below the blue-gray band

**Juvenile:** similar to female

**Nest:** cavity; female and male excavate in a bank of a river, lake or cliff; 1 brood per year

**Eggs:** 6–7; white without markings

**Incubation:** 23–24 days; female and male incubate

**Fledging:** 23–24 days; female and male feed the young

**Migration:** complete to non-migrator in Florida

**Food:** small fish

**Compare:** The Blue Jay (p. 109) is lighter blue and has a plain gray chest and belly. The Belted Kingfisher is rarely found away from water.

**Stan's Notes:** Usually found at the bank of a river, lake or large stream. Perches on a branch near water, dives in headfirst to catch a small fish, then returns to the branch to feed. Parents drop dead fish into the water to teach their young to dive. Can't pass bones through its digestive tract; regurgitates bone pellets after meals. Gives a loud call that sounds like a machine gun. Mates know each other by their calls. Digs a tunnel up to 4 feet (1 m) long to a nest chamber. Small white patches on dark wing tips flash during flight.

# Purple Gallinule
*Porphyrio martinicus*

YEAR-ROUND
SUMMER

**Size:** 13" (33 cm)

**Male:** A vibrant blue head, breast and belly with iridescent green back and wings. Yellow-tipped red bill. White undertail. Yellow legs.

**Female:** same as male

**Juvenile:** brown version of adult, bronze legs

**Nest:** ground; female and male build; 1–2 broods per year

**Eggs:** 6–8; brown with dark markings

**Incubation:** 22–25 days; female and male incubate

**Fledging:** 55–60 days; female and male feed the young

**Migration:** parital to non-migrator in Florida

**Food:** insects, snails, seeds, berries, frogs

**Compare:** American Coot (p. 35) is similar in size but is black and lacks a yellow-tipped red bill. Common Gallinule (p. 33) is a similar size, but it has a white side stripe and lacks the green back. Look for a white undertail to help identify the Purple Gallinule.

**Stan's Notes:** This is one of Florida's most dramatic-looking birds, commonly seen in the Everglades. Uses its extremely long toes to walk on floating vegetation in freshwater and saltwater marshes, where it hunts for grasshoppers and other insects, seeds and frogs. Family groups stay together; first brood sometimes helps raise the second. Moves out of northern Florida during winter and can be seen year-round in the southern part of the state. Individuals are known to wander well north of Florida.

non-breeding

breeding

molting
juvenile

white
juvenile

YEAR-ROUND
SUMMER

# Little Blue Heron
*Egretta caerulea*

**Size:** 22–26" (56–66 cm)

**Male:** Dark slate-blue to purple nearly all year. Dull-green legs and feet. Black-tipped blue-gray bill. Breeding adult has a reddish-purple head and neck with several long plumes on the crown.

**Female:** same as male

**Juvenile:** pure white overall, yellowish legs and feet, black-tipped gray bill

**Nest:** platform; female and male build; 1 brood per year

**Eggs:** 2–6; light blue without markings

**Incubation:** 20–23 days; female and male incubate

**Fledging:** 42–49 days; female and male feed the young

**Migration:** non-migrator to partial in Florida

**Food:** fish, aquatic insects

**Compare:** Tricolored Heron (p. 117) has a white belly. Snowy Egret (p. 339) can be confused with a juvenile Little Blue, but Snowy has bright-yellow feet, black legs and a solid black bill. The breeding Cattle Egret (p. 337) has an orange-buff crest, breast and back, and a red-orange bill.

**Stan's Notes:** Unusual because the young look completely different from adults. All-white young turn blotchy white the first year. By the second year they look like the adult birds. A very slow stalker of prey in freshwater lakes and rivers, saltwater marshes and wetlands. Nests in large colonies near saltwater sites. Some fly north after breeding, returning to Florida for the winter.

**115**

breeding

non-breeding

# Tricolored Heron
*Egretta tricolor*

YEAR-ROUND
SUMMER

**Size:** 24–28" (60–71 cm)

**Male:** Dark-blue head, wings and back of neck. White belly and white stripe on underside of neck. Small brown patches at base of neck, with lighter brown on the lower back. Legs are yellow to pale green. Long, slender bill with a dark tip.

**Female:** same as male

**Juvenile:** similar to adult, chestnut-brown in place of dark-blue areas

**Nest:** platform; female and male build; 1 brood per year

**Eggs:** 3–6; light blue without markings

**Incubation:** 21–25 days; female and male incubate

**Fledging:** 32–35 days; female and male feed the young

**Migration:** non-migrator to partial in Florida

**Food:** fish, aquatic insects

**Compare:** Great Blue Heron (p. 291) is much larger and lacks white undersides. The Little Blue Heron (p. 115) is slightly smaller and lacks the yellow bill and white belly.

**Stan's Notes:** A medium-sized heron characterized by its white undersides. Like other herons, numbers have declined due to habitat loss. To hunt, it stands still and waits. Will also chase small fish. A year-round resident, although less numerous in summer. Seen mainly in saltwater marshes and estuaries, but also in freshwater marshes inland. In spring and summer, known to wander as far as Kansas. Colony nester with other herons, one adult always on duty at the nest. Was not hunted for plumes like other herons.

white
morph

dark morph

hunting

# Reddish Egret
*Egretta rufescens*

YEAR-ROUND

**Size:** 30" (76 cm)

**Male:** A slate-blue-bodied egret with a shaggy reddish head and neck. Long dark legs and feet. Long, pointed black-tipped bill. White morph is all white with shaggy plumes at base of neck and a dark-tipped pink bill.

**Female:** same as male

**Juvenile:** pale version of adult

**Nest:** platform; female and male build; 1 brood per year

**Eggs:** 3–4; light blue without markings

**Incubation:** 25–26 days; female and male incubate

**Fledging:** 42–46 days; female and male feed young

**Migration:** non-migrator; moves around to find food

**Food:** fish, aquatic insects

**Compare:** Tricolored Heron (p. 117) is smaller, has a white belly and lacks the reddish head and neck. The Little Blue Heron (p. 115) has a blue-gray bill with a dark tip. Snowy Egret (p. 339) has yellow feet and a yellow mark at the base of its bill.

**Stan's Notes:** Inhabits saltwater on the coast. "Dances" in shallow water, hunting. Two color morphs, with the dark morph more common than the white. Identified by its unusual hunting behavior. Runs with wings open to shade water, darting its head to grab a fish. May stir the bottom with its feet to expose fish. Nearly eliminated by plume hunters by the late 1800s. Populations have rebounded, but the species remains uncommon. Often alone and silent. May croak or bark upon takeoff when disturbed.

# Chimney Swift
*Chaetura pelagica*

**Size:** 5" (13 cm)

**Male:** Nondescript, cigar-shaped bird, usually seen in flight. Long, thin, brown body. Pointed tail and head. Long, backswept wings, longer than the body.

**Female:** same as male

**Juvenile:** same as adult

**Nest:** half cup; female and male build; 1 brood per year

**Eggs:** 4–5; white without markings

**Incubation:** 19–21 days; female and male incubate

**Fledging:** 28–30 days; female and male feed the young

**Migration:** complete, to South America

**Food:** insects caught in midair

**Compare:** The Purple Martin (p. 105) is much larger and darker. The Barn Swallow (p. 101) has a deeply forked tail. Tree Swallows (p. 99) have a white belly and blue-green back. Look for the cigar shape to identify the Chimney Swift in flight.

**Stan's Notes:** One of the fastest fliers in the bird world. Spends all day flying, rarely perching. Flies in groups, feeding on insects flying 100 feet (30 m) or higher up in the air. Often called a Flying Cigar due to its body shape, which is pointed at both ends. Drinks and bathes during flight, skimming water. Gives a unique in-flight twittering call, often heard before the bird is seen. Hundreds roost in large chimneys, giving it the common name. Builds its nest with tiny twigs, cementing it with saliva and attaching it to the inside of a chimney or a hollow tree. Usually only one nest per chimney.

# Chipping Sparrow
*Spizella passerina*

YEAR-ROUND
WINTER

| | |
|---|---|
| **Size:** | 5" (13 cm) |
| **Male:** | Small gray-brown sparrow with clear-gray chest. Rusty crown. White eyebrows and thin black eye line. Thin gray-black bill. Two faint wing bars. |
| **Female:** | same as male |
| **Juvenile:** | similar to adults, with streaking on the chest; lacks a rusty crown |
| **Nest:** | cup; female builds; 2 broods per year |
| **Eggs:** | 3–5; blue-green with brown markings |
| **Incubation:** | 11–14 days; female incubates |
| **Fledging:** | 10–12 days; female and male feed the young |
| **Migration:** | complete, to Florida, other southern states, Mexico and Central America |
| **Food:** | insects, seeds; will come to ground feeders |
| **Compare:** | The Song Sparrow (p. 133) and female House Finch (p. 315) have heavily streaked chests. Look for the rusty crown and black eye line to help identify the Chipping Sparrow. |

**Stan's Notes:** A winter resident in Florida, seen from October to May. A common garden or yard bird, often seen feeding on dropped seeds beneath feeders. Gathers in large family groups to feed in preparation for migration. Migrates at night in flocks of 20–30 birds. The common name comes from the male's fast "chip" call. Often is just called Chippy. Builds nest low in dense shrubs and almost always lines it with animal hair. Comfortable with people, allowing you to approach closely before it flies away.

male
p. 315

female

# House Finch
*Haemorhous mexicanus*

YEAR-ROUND

**Size:** 5" (13 cm)

**Female:** Plain brown with heavy streaking on a white chest.

**Male:** red-to-orange face, throat, chest and rump; streaked belly and wings; brown cap; brown marking behind the eyes

**Juvenile:** similar to female

**Nest:** cup, occasionally in a cavity; female builds; 2 broods per year

**Eggs:** 4–5; pale blue, lightly marked

**Incubation:** 12–14 days; female incubates

**Fledging:** 15–19 days; female and male feed the young

**Migration:** non-migrator to partial migrator; will move around to find food

**Food:** seeds, fruit, leaf buds; visits seed feeders and feeders that offer grape jelly

**Compare:** The female Purple Finch (p. 137) has bold white eyebrows. The female American Goldfinch (p. 351) has a clear chest. Look for the heavily streaked chest to help identify the female House Finch.

**Stan's Notes:** Can be a common bird at your feeders. A very social bird, visiting feeders in small flocks. Likes to nest in hanging flower baskets. Male sings a loud, cheerful warbling song. It was originally introduced to Long Island, New York, from the western U.S. in the 1940s. Now found throughout the country. Suffers from a disease that causes the eyes to crust, resulting in blindness and death.

# House Wren
*Troglodytes aedon*

WINTER

**Size:** 5" (13 cm)

**Male:** All-brown bird with lighter-brown markings on the wings and tail. Slightly curved brown bill. Often holds tail upward.

**Female:** same as male

**Juvenile:** same as adult

**Nest:** cavity; female and male line just about any nest cavity; 2 broods per year

**Eggs:** 4–6; tan with brown markings

**Incubation:** 10–13 days; female and male incubate

**Fledging:** 12–15 days; female and male feed the young

**Migration:** complete, to Florida, other southern states and Mexico

**Food:** insects, spiders, snails

**Compare:** Carolina Wren (p. 129) has prominent eyebrows. Look for House Wren's long curved bill and long upturned tail to differentiate it from sparrows.

**Stan's Notes:** A prolific songster. During the mating season, sings from dawn to dusk. Seen in brushy yards, parks and woodlands and along forest edges. Easily attracted to a nest box. In spring, the male chooses several prospective nesting cavities and places a few small twigs in each. The female inspects all of them and finishes constructing the nest in the cavity of her choice. She fills the cavity with short twigs and then lines a small depression at the back with pine needles and grass. She often has trouble fitting longer twigs through the entrance hole and tries many different directions and approaches until she is successful.

YEAR-ROUND

# Carolina Wren
*Thryothorus ludovicianus*

**Size:** 5½" (14 cm)

**Male:** Rusty-brown head and back with an orange-yellow chest and belly. White throat and a prominent white eye stripe. Short, stubby tail, often cocked up.

**Female:** same as male

**Juvenile:** same as adults

**Nest:** cavity; female and male build; 2 broods per year, sometimes 3

**Eggs:** 4–6; white, sometimes pink or creamy, with brown markings

**Incubation:** 12–14 days; female incubates

**Fledging:** 12–14 days; female and male feed the young

**Migration:** non-migrator

**Food:** insects, fruit, few seeds; visits suet feeders

**Compare:** House Wren (p. 127) is darker brown and lacks a white eye stripe.

**Stan's Notes:** Mates are long-term, staying together throughout the year in permanent territories. Sings year-round. The male is known to sing up to 40 song types, singing one song repeatedly before switching to another. The female also sings, resulting in duets. The male often takes over feeding the first brood while the female renests. Nests in birdhouses and in unusual places like mailboxes, bumpers or broken taillights of vehicles, or nearly any other cavity. Found in brushy yards or woodlands. Can be attracted to feeders with mealworms.

female

male
p. 97

SUMMER
MIGRATION
WINTER

# Indigo Bunting
*Passerina cyanea*

**Size:** 5½" (14 cm)

**Female:** Light-brown, finch-like bird. Faint streaking on a light-tan chest. Wings have a very faint blue cast and indistinct wing bars.

**Male:** vibrant blue with scattered dark markings on wings and tail

**Juvenile:** similar to female

**Nest:** cup; female builds; 2 broods per year

**Eggs:** 3–4; pale blue without markings

**Incubation:** 12–13 days; female incubates

**Fledging:** 10–11 days; female feeds the young

**Migration:** complete, to southern Florida, Mexico, Central America and South America

**Food:** insects, seeds, fruit; will visit seed feeders

**Compare:** The female Purple Finch (p. 137) has white eyebrows and heavy streaking on the chest. The female House Finch (p. 125) has a heavily streaked chest. The female American Goldfinch (p. 351) has white wing bars. Look for the faint blue cast on the wings to help identify the female Indigo Bunting.

**Stan's Notes:** Seen along woodland edges and in parks and yards, feeding on insects. Comes to seed feeders early in spring, before insects are plentiful. Secretive, plain and quiet; usually only the males are noticed. The male often sings from treetops to attract a mate. Migrates at night in flocks of 5–10 birds. Males return before the females and juveniles, often to the nest site of the preceding year. Juveniles move to within a mile of their birth site.

# Song Sparrow

*Melospiza melodia*

WINTER

**Size:** 5–6" (13–15 cm)

**Male:** Common brown sparrow with heavy dark streaks on the chest coalescing into a central dark spot.

**Female:** same as male

**Juvenile:** similar to adults, with a finely streaked chest; lacks a central dark spot

**Nest:** cup; female builds; 2 broods per year

**Eggs:** 3–4; blue to green, with red-brown markings

**Incubation:** 12–14 days; female incubates

**Fledging:** 9–12 days; female and male feed the young

**Migration:** complete, to Florida, other southern states

**Food:** insects, seeds; only rarely comes to ground feeders with seeds

**Compare:** Similar to other brown sparrows. Look for the heavily streaked chest with a central dark spot to help identify the Song Sparrow.

**Stan's Notes:** There are many subspecies of this bird, but the dark spot in the center of the chest appears in every variety. A constant songster, repeating its loud, clear song every few minutes. The song varies from region to region but has the same basic structure. Sings from thick shrubs to defend a small territory, beginning with three notes and finishing up with a trill. A ground feeder, it will "double-scratch" with both feet at the same time to expose seeds. When the female builds a new nest for a second brood, the male often takes over feeding the first brood. Unlike many other sparrow species, Song Sparrows rarely flock together. A common host of the Brown-headed Cowbird.

male

female

# House Sparrow
*Passer domesticus*

YEAR-ROUND

| | |
|---|---|
| **Size:** | 6" (15 cm) |
| **Male:** | Brown back with a gray belly and cap. Large black patch extending from the throat to the chest (bib). One white wing bar. |
| **Female:** | slightly smaller than the male; light brown with light eyebrows; lacks a bib and white wing bar |
| **Juvenile:** | similar to female |
| **Nest:** | cavity; female and male build a domed cup nest within; 2–3 broods per year |
| **Eggs:** | 4–6; white with brown markings |
| **Incubation:** | 10–12 days; female incubates |
| **Fledging:** | 14–17 days; female and male feed the young |
| **Migration:** | non-migrator; moves around to find food |
| **Food:** | seeds, insects, fruit; comes to seed feeders |
| **Compare:** | Chipping Sparrow (p. 123) has a rusty crown. Look for the black bib to identify the male House Sparrow and the clear breast to help identify the female. |

**Stan's Notes:** One of the first birdsongs heard in cities in spring. A familiar city bird, nearly always in small flocks. Also found on farms. Introduced in 1850 from Europe to Central Park in New York. Now seen throughout North America. Related to old-world sparrows; not a relative of any sparrows in the U.S. An aggressive bird that will kill young birds in order to take over the nest cavity. Uses dried grass and small scraps of plastic, paper and other materials to build an oversize, domed nest in the cavity.

male
p. 317

female

WINTER

# Purple Finch
*Haemorhous purpureus*

**Size:** 6" (15 cm)

**Female:** Plain brown with heavy streaking on the chest. Bold white eyebrows and a large bill.

**Male:** raspberry-red head, cap, breast, back and rump; brownish wings and tail

**Juvenile:** same as female

**Nest:** cup; female and male build; 1 brood per year

**Eggs:** 4–5; greenish blue with brown markings

**Incubation:** 12–13 days; female incubates

**Fledging:** 13–14 days; female and male feed the young

**Migration:** irruptive; moves around in winter in search of food

**Food:** seeds, insects, fruit; comes to seed feeders

**Compare:** The female House Finch (p. 125) lacks eyebrows. The female American Goldfinch (p. 351) has a clear chest. Look for the bold white eyebrows to identify the female Purple Finch.

**Stan's Notes:** Usually seen only during the winter in northern Florida, when flocks of Purple Finches leave their homes farther north and move around searching for food. Travels in flocks of up to 50 birds. Visits seed feeders along with House Finches, which makes it hard to tell them apart. Feeds mainly on seeds; ash tree seeds are an important source of food. Found in coniferous forests, mixed woods, woodland edges and suburban backyards. Flies in the typical undulating, up-and-down pattern of finches. Sings a rich, loud song. Gives a distinctive "tic" note only in flight. The male is not purple. The Latin species name *purpureus* means "purple" (and other reddish colors).

winter p. 237

breeding

# Least Sandpiper
*Calidris minutilla*

MIGRATION
WINTER

**Size:** 6" (15 cm)

**Male:** Breeding plumage has a golden-brown head and back and a white belly. Dull-yellow legs. White eyebrows and a short, down-curved black bill.

**Female:** same as male

**Juvenile:** similar to winter adult but buff-brown and lacks the breast band

**Nest:** ground; male and female construct; 1 brood per year

**Eggs:** 3–4; olive with dark markings

**Incubation:** 19–23 days; male and female incubate

**Fledging:** 25–28 days; male and female feed the young

**Migration:** complete, to coastal Florida, other southern coastal states, Mexico and Central America

**Food:** aquatic and terrestrial insects, seeds

**Compare:** The smallest of sandpipers. Often confused with breeding Western Sandpiper (p. 141) and Semipalmated Sandpiper (p. 239), look for Least Sandpiper's yellow legs to differentiate it from other tiny sandpipers. The short, thin down-curved bill also helps to identify.

**Stan's Notes:** A winter resident in coastal Florida. Also winters in southern coastal states from the Carolinas to California. This is a tiny, tame sandpiper that can be approached without scaring it. It is the smallest of peeps (sandpipers), nesting on the tundra in northern regions of Canada and Alaska. Prefers the grassy flats of saltwater and freshwater ponds. Its yellow legs can be hard to see in water, poor light or when covered with mud.

**139**

winter p. 241

breeding

# Western Sandpiper
*Calidris mauri*

MIGRATION
WINTER

| | |
|---|---|
| **Size:** | 6½" (16 cm) |
| **Male:** | Breeding has a bright rust-brown crown, ear patch and back and a white chin and chest. Black legs. Narrow bill that droops near tip. |
| **Female:** | same as male |
| **Juvenile:** | similar to breeding adult; bright buff-brown on the back only |
| **Nest:** | ground; male and female construct; 1 brood per year |
| **Eggs:** | 2–4; light brown with dark markings |
| **Incubation:** | 20–22 days; male and female incubate |
| **Fledging:** | 19–21 days; male and female feed the young |
| **Migration:** | complete, to coastal Florida |
| **Food:** | aquatic and terrestrial insects |
| **Compare:** | Breeding Least Sandpiper (p. 139) and Semipalmated Sandpiper (p. 239) lack the bright rust-brown cap, ear patch and back. Least Sandpiper has yellow legs. Look for Western's longer bill that droops slightly at the tip. |

**Stan's Notes:** A winter resident in coastal Florida. Also winters in southern coastal states from the Carolinas to California. Nests on the ground in large "loose" colonies on the tundra of northern coastal Alaska. Adults leave their breeding grounds several weeks before the young. Some obtain their breeding plumage before leaving in spring. Feeds on insects at the water's edge, sometimes immersing its head. Feeds in deeper water than the Semipalmated Sandpiper. Young leave the nest (precocial) within a few hours after hatching. Female leaves and the male tends the hatchlings.

winter

breeding

# Semipalmated Plover
*Charadrius semipalmatus*

MIGRATION
WINTER

**Size:** 7" (18 cm)

**Male:** A brown-backed bird with a white breast and belly. Black crown, mask and necklace. White patch on forehead. Orange eye-ring. Yellow legs. Short, black-tipped orange bill. Winter plumage has a brown mask and lacks the orange eye-ring.

**Female:** same as male

**Juvenile:** similar to adult but lacks a well-defined black necklace

**Nest:** ground; male builds; 1 brood per year

**Eggs:** 3–4; light brown with dark markings

**Incubation:** 23–25 days; male and female incubate

**Fledging:** 22–28 days; male and female feed the young

**Migration:** complete, to coastal Florida

**Food:** insects, seeds, worms

**Compare:** Killdeer (p. 173) shares the brown back and white belly, but it is larger and has 2 black neck bands. Look for a very short bill and single black necklace to help identify the Semipalmated Plover.

**Stan's Notes:** Winter resident along coastal Florida. Also winters in southern coastal states from the Carolinas to California. Often in mixed flocks with Semipalmated Sandpipers. Hunts by running quickly, stopping to look, then stabbing its prey. Breeding birds often have orange eye-rings. Prefers to nest in open rocky places, where the male will scrape out a shallow depression. Nests on the ground on the tundra of northern Canada and Alaska.

female

male
p. 23

# Eastern Towhee
*Pipilo erythrophthalmus*

YEAR-ROUND

**Size:** 7–8" (18–20 cm)

**Female:** Mostly light-brown bird. Rusty red-brown sides and a white belly. Long brown tail with a white tip. Short, stout, pointed bill and off-white eyes. White wing patches flash in flight.

**Male:** similar to female but black instead of brown

**Juvenile:** Light brown with a heavily streaked head, chest and belly. Long dark tail with a white tip.

**Nest:** cup; female builds; 2 broods per year

**Eggs:** 3–4; creamy white with brown markings

**Incubation:** 12–13 days; female incubates

**Fledging:** 10–12 days; male and female feed the young

**Migration:** non-migrator in Florida

**Food:** insects, seeds, fruit; visits ground feeders

**Compare:** The American Robin (p. 261) is larger, has a red breast and lacks the white belly.

**Stan's Notes:** Named for its distinctive "tow-hee" call, given by both sexes, but known mostly for its other characteristic call, which sounds like "drink-your-tea!" Will hop backward with both feet (double-scratching), raking up leaf litter to locate insects and seeds. The female does the brooding. The male feeds the young most of the time. In southern coastal states, some have red eyes; others have white eyes. The white-eyed variety is found in Florida.

male
p. 25

female

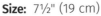

# Brown-headed Cowbird
*Molothrus ater*

**YEAR-ROUND**

**Size:** 7½" (19 cm)

**Female:** Dull brown with no obvious markings. Pointed, sharp, gray bill. Dark eyes.

**Male:** glossy black with a chocolate-brown head

**Juvenile:** similar to female but with dull-gray plumage and a streaked chest

**Nest:** no nest; lays eggs in the nests of other birds

**Eggs:** 5–7; white with brown markings

**Incubation:** 10–13 days; host bird incubates the eggs

**Fledging:** 10–11 days; host birds feed the young

**Migration:** non-migrator in Florida

**Food:** insects, seeds; will come to seed feeders

**Compare:** The female Red-winged Blackbird (p. 159) has white eyebrows and heavy streaking. The female Indigo Bunting (p. 131) has faint blue on its wings. The pointed gray bill helps to identify the female Brown-headed Cowbird.

**Stan's Notes:** Cowbirds are members of the blackbird family. Known as brood parasites, Brown-headed Cowbirds are the only parasitic birds in Florida. Brood parasites lay their eggs in the nests of other birds, leaving the host birds to raise their young. Cowbirds are known to have laid their eggs in the nests of over 200 species of birds. While some birds reject cowbird eggs, most incubate them and raise the young, even to the exclusion of their own. Look for warblers and other birds feeding young birds twice their own size. Named "Cowbird" for its habit of following bison and cattle herds to feed on insects flushed up by the animals.

1 year
old

# Cedar Waxwing
*Bombycilla cedrorum*

WINTER

| | |
|---|---|
| **Size:** | 7½" (19 cm) |
| **Male:** | Sleek-looking, gray-to-brown bird. Pointed crest, bandit-like mask and light-yellow belly. Bold-yellow tip of tail. Red wing tips look like they were dipped in red wax. |
| **Female:** | same as male |
| **Juvenile:** | grayish with a heavily streaked breast; lacks the sleek look, black mask and red wing tips |
| **Nest:** | cup; female and male construct; 1 brood per year, occasionally 2 |
| **Eggs:** | 4–6; pale blue with brown markings |
| **Incubation:** | 10–12 days; female incubates |
| **Fledging:** | 14–18 days; female and male feed the young |
| **Migration:** | partial migrator; moves around to find food |
| **Food:** | cedar cones, fruit, insects |
| **Compare:** | The female Northern Cardinal (p. 157) has a large red bill. Look for the red wing tips to identify the Cedar Waxwing. |

**Stan's Notes:** The name is derived from its red, wax-like wing tips and preference for the small, berry-like cones of the cedar. Seen in flocks, moving around from area to area looking for berries. Feeds on insects during summer, before berries are abundant. Wanders during winter, searching for food supplies. Spends most of its time at the top of tall trees. Listen for the high-pitched "sreee" whistling sound it constantly makes while perched or in flight. Obtains the mask after the first year and red wing tips after the second year.

winter

breeding

# Spotted Sandpiper

*Actitis macularius*

MIGRATION
WINTER

**Size:** 8" (20 cm)

**Male:** Olive-brown back with black spots on a white chest and belly. White line over eyes. Long, dull-yellow legs. Long bill. Winter plumage lacks spots on the chest and belly.

**Female:** same as male

**Juvenile:** similar to winter plumage, with a darker bill

**Nest:** ground; male builds; 2 broods per year

**Eggs:** 3–4; brownish with brown markings

**Incubation:** 20–24 days; male incubates

**Fledging:** 17–21 days; male feeds the young

**Migration:** complete, to coastal Florida

**Food:** aquatic insects

**Compare:** Lesser Yellowlegs (p. 169) is larger. Killdeer (p. 173) has 2 black neck bands. Look for the black spots on the chest and belly and the bobbing tail to help identify the breeding Spotted Sandpiper.

**Stan's Notes:** This is one of the more common sandpipers. Seen along the shorelines of large ponds, lakes and rivers. One of the few shorebirds that will dive underwater when pursued. Able to fly straight up out of the water. Holds wings in a cup-like arc in flight, rarely lifting them above a horizontal plane. Walks as if delicately balanced. When standing, constantly bobs its tail. Gives a rapid series of "weet-weet-weet" calls when frightened and flying away. Female mates with multiple males and lays eggs in up to five nests. Male does all of the nest building, incubating and childcare without any help from the female.

winter
p. 251

breeding

MIGRATION
WINTER

# Sanderling
*Calidris alba*

**Size:** 8" (20 cm)

**Male:** Breeding adult (April to August) has a rusty head, chest and back with white belly. Black legs and bill.

**Female:** same as male

**Juvenile:** spotty black on the head and back, a white belly, black legs and bill

**Nest:** ground; male builds; 1–2 broods per year

**Eggs:** 3–4; greenish olive with brown markings

**Incubation:** 24–30 days; male and female incubate

**Fledging:** 16–17 days; female and male feed the young

**Migration:** complete, to coastal Florida, other southern coastal states, Mexico and Central America

**Food:** insects

**Compare:** Spotted Sandpiper (p. 151) is the same size as Sanderling, but the breeding Spotted Sandpiper has black spots on its chest.

**Stan's Notes:** One of the most common shorebirds in Florida, but mostly seen in its gray winter plumage from August to April. Can be seen in groups on sandy beaches, running out with each retreating wave to feed. Look for a flash of white on the wings when it is in flight. Sometimes a female will mate with several males (polyandry), which results in males and the female incubating separate nests. Both sexes perform a distraction display if threatened. Nests on the Arctic tundra. Rests by standing on one leg (see inset) and tucking the other leg into its belly feathers. Often hops away on one leg, moving away from pedestrians on the beach. Surveys show a greater than 80 percent decline in numbers since the 1970s.

winter
p. 253

breeding

# Dunlin
*Calidris alpina*

MIGRATION
WINTER

**Size:** 8–9" (20–23 cm)

**Male:** Breeding adult is distinctive with a rusty-red back, finely streaked chest and an obvious black patch on the belly. Stout bill, curving slightly downward at the tip. Black legs.

**Female:** slightly larger than male, with a longer bill

**Juvenile:** slightly rusty back with a spotty chest

**Nest:** ground; male and female construct; 1 brood per year

**Eggs:** 2–4; olive-buff or blue-green with red-brown markings

**Incubation:** 21–22 days; male incubates during the day, female incubates at night

**Fledging:** 19–21 days; male feeds the young, female often leaves before the young fledge

**Migration:** complete, to coastal Florida, other southern coastal states, Mexico and Central America

**Food:** insects

**Compare:** Breeding Sanderling (p. 153) is similar in size, but look for the obvious black belly patch and curved bill of breeding Dunlin.

**Stan's Notes:** Breeding plumage more commonly seen in spring. Flights include heights of up to 100 feet (30 m) with brief gliding alternating with shallow flutters, and a rhythmic, repeating song. Huge flocks fly synchronously, with birds twisting and turning, flashing light and dark undersides. Males tend to fly farther south in winter than females. Winter visitor along the coast. Doesn't nest in Florida.

male
p. 321

female

juvenile

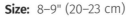

# Northern Cardinal

*Cardinalis cardinalis*

**Size:** 8–9" (20–23 cm)

**Female:** Buff-brown with red tinges on the crest and wings. Black mask and a large reddish bill.

**Male:** red with a large crest and bill and a black mask extending from the face to the throat

**Juvenile:** same as female but with a blackish-gray bill

**Nest:** cup; female builds; 2–3 broods per year

**Eggs:** 3–4; bluish white with brown markings

**Incubation:** 12–13 days; female and male incubate

**Fledging:** 9–10 days; female and male feed the young

**Migration:** non-migrator

**Food:** seeds, insects, fruit; comes to seed feeders

**Compare:** The Cedar Waxwing (p. 149) has a small dark bill. The juvenile Northern Cardinal (bottom inset) looks like the adult female but with a dark bill. Look for the reddish bill to identify the female Northern Cardinal.

**Stan's Notes:** A familiar backyard bird. Seen in a variety of habitats, including parks. Usually likes thick vegetation. One of the few species in which both females and males sing. Can be heard all year. Listen for its "whata-cheer-cheer-cheer" territorial call in spring. Watch for a male feeding a female during courtship. The male also feeds the young of the first brood while the female builds a second nest. Territorial in spring, fighting its own reflection in a window or other reflective surface. Non-territorial in winter, gathering in small flocks of up to 20 birds. Makes short flights from cover to cover, often landing on the ground. *Cardinalis* denotes importance, as represented by the red priestly garments of Catholic cardinals.

male
p. 29

female

# Red-winged Blackbird
*Agelaius phoeniceus*

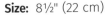

YEAR-ROUND

**Size:** 8½" (22 cm)

**Female:** Heavily streaked brown body. Pointed brown bill and white eyebrows.

**Male:** jet black with red-and-yellow shoulder patches (epaulets) and a pointed black bill

**Juvenile:** same as female

**Nest:** cup; female builds; 2–3 broods per year

**Eggs:** 3–4; bluish green with brown markings

**Incubation:** 10–12 days; female incubates

**Fledging:** 11–14 days; female and male feed the young

**Migration:** partial to non-migrator in Florida

**Food:** seeds, insects; visits seed and suet feeders

**Compare:** The female Brown-headed Cowbird (p. 147) lacks streaks. Look for white eyebrows and heavy streaking to identify the female Red-winged.

**Stan's Notes:** One of the most widespread and numerous birds in Florida. In fall and winter, migrant and resident Red-wingeds gather in huge numbers (thousands) with other blackbirds to feed in agricultural fields, marshes and wetlands. Found around marshes, wetlands, lakes and rivers. Flocks with as many as 10,000 birds have been reported. Males arrive before females and sing to defend their territory. The male repeats his call from the top of a cattail while showing off his red-and-yellow shoulder patches. The female chooses a mate and often builds her nest over shallow water in a thick stand of cattails. The male can be aggressive when defending the nest. Feeds mostly on seeds in spring and fall, and insects throughout the summer.

female

male

# Common Nighthawk
*Chordeiles minor*

SUMMER

**Size:** 9" (23 cm)

**Male:** Camouflaged brown and white with a white chin. Distinctive white band across the wings and tail, seen only in flight.

**Female:** similar to male, with a tan chin; lacks a white tail band

**Juvenile:** similar to female

**Nest:** no nest; lays eggs on the ground, usually on rocks, or on rooftop; 1 brood per year

**Eggs:** 2; cream with lavender markings

**Incubation:** 19–20 days; female and male incubate

**Fledging:** 20–21 days; female and male feed the young

**Migration:** complete, to South America

**Food:** insects caught in the air

**Compare:** The Chimney Swift (p. 121) is much smaller. Look for the white chin, obvious white band on the wings and characteristic flap-flap-flap-glide pattern to help identify the Common Nighthawk.

**Stan's Notes:** Usually only seen in flight at dusk or after sunset but not uncommon to see it sleeping on a branch during the day. A prolific insect eater and very noisy in flight, repeating a "peenting" call. Alternates slow wingbeats with bursts of quick wingbeats. In cities, prefers to nest on flat rooftops with gravel. City populations are on the decline as gravel rooftops are converted to other styles. In spring, the male performs a showy mating ritual consisting of a steep diving flight ending with a loud popping noise. One of the first birds to migrate in fall. Often seen in large flocks.

# Burrowing Owl
*Athene cunicularia*

YEAR-ROUND

**Size:** 9–10" (24 cm); up to 2' wingspan

**Male:** A brown owl with bold white spots and a white belly. Yellow eyes and very long legs.

**Female:** same as male

**Juvenile:** same as adult, but belly is brown

**Nest:** cavity, former underground mammal den; female and male line den; 1 brood per year

**Eggs:** 6–11; white without markings

**Incubation:** 26–30 days; female incubates

**Fledging:** 25–28 days; female and male feed young

**Migration:** non-migrator in southern Florida

**Food:** insects, mammals, lizards, birds

**Compare:** Eastern Screech-Owl (p. 255) is slightly smaller and has ear tufts. Burrowing Owl is less than half the size of Great Horned Owl (p. 219) is more than twice the size of Burrowing and has feather tuft "horns." Burrowing spends most of its time on the ground, unlike tree-loving Great Horned.

**Stan's Notes:** An owl of fields, open backyards, golf courses and airports. Nests in large family units or in small colonies. Takes over the underground dens of mammals, occasionally widening its den by kicking dirt backward. Lines den with cow pies, horse dung, grass and feathers. Some people have had success attracting these owls to their backyards by creating artificial dens. Often seen during the day, standing or sleeping around den entrance. Male brings food to incubating female, often moving family to a new den when young are just a few weeks old. Will bob head up and down while doing deep knee bends when agitated or threatened.

in flight

juvenile

male

female

in-flight juvenile

# American Kestrel
*Falco sparverius*

YEAR-ROUND

**Size:** 9–11" (23–28 cm); up to 2' wingspan

**Male:** Rust-brown back and tail. White breast with dark spots. Two vertical black lines on a white face. Blue-gray wings. Wide black band with a white edge on the tip of a rusty tail.

**Female:** similar to male but slightly larger, with rust-brown wings and dark bands on the tail

**Juvenile:** same as adult of the same sex

**Nest:** cavity; does not build a nest; 1 brood per year

**Eggs:** 4–5; white with brown markings

**Incubation:** 29–31 days; male and female incubate

**Fledging:** 30–31 days; female and male feed the young

**Migration:** complete to non-migrator in Florida

**Food:** insects, small mammals and birds, reptiles

**Compare:** The Peregrine Falcon (p. 283) is much larger and has a dark "hood" marking. No other small bird of prey has a rusty back and tail.

**Stan's Notes:** An unusual raptor because the sexes look different (dimorphic). Due to its small size, this falcon was once called a Sparrow Hawk. Hovers near roads, then dives for prey. Watch for it to pump its tail after landing on a perch. Perches nearly upright. Eats many grasshoppers. Adapts quickly to a wooden nest box. Can be extremely vocal, giving a loud series of high-pitched calls. Ability to see ultraviolet (UV) light helps it locate mice and other prey by their urine, which glows bright yellow in UV light.

male

female

# Northern Bobwhite
*Colinus virginianus*

YEAR-ROUND

**Size:** 10" (25 cm)

**Male:** Short, stocky and mostly brown with short gray tail. Prominent white eye stripe and white chin. Reddish-brown sides and belly, often with black lines and dots.

**Female:** similar to male, with buff-brown eye stripe and chin

**Juvenile:** smaller and duller than adults

**Nest:** ground; female and male construct; 1 brood per year

**Eggs:** 12–15; white to creamy without markings

**Incubation:** 23–24 days; female and male incubate

**Fledging:** 6–7 days; female and male feed the young

**Migration:** non-migrator

**Food:** insects, seeds, fruit; will come to ground feeders offering corn and millet

**Compare:** Mourning Dove (p. 179) is light brown and has a long pointed tail. Look for a small chicken-shaped bird, usually seen in small groups.

**Stan's Notes:** Most common in northern Florida. Prefers shrubs, orchards, hedgerows and pastures. Moves around in small flocks of 20 birds (often family members), called a covey. The covey often rests together during the night, in a tight circle with tails together and heads facing outward, to watch for predators. Males and females perform distraction displays when nests or young are threatened. Nest is a depression in the ground lined with grass. Often pulls nearby vegetation over nest to help conceal it. Male gives a rising whistle, "bob-white," heard mainly in spring and summer. Also gives a single "hoy" call year-round.

# Lesser Yellowlegs
*Tringa flavipes*

MIGRATION
WINTER

**Size:** 10–12" (25–30 cm)

**Male:** A typical sandpiper-type bird with a brown back and wings, and a streaked white chest. Thin, straight black bill. Long yellow legs.

**Female:** same as male

**Juvenile:** same as adult

**Nest:** ground; female builds; 1 brood per year

**Eggs:** 3–4; yellowish with brown markings

**Incubation:** 22–23 days; male and female incubate

**Fledging:** 18–20 days; male and female lead the young to food

**Migration:** complete, to Florida and South America

**Food:** aquatic insects, tiny fish

**Compare:** Greater Yellowlegs (p. 183) is much larger and has a longer, slightly upturned bill. Breeding Willet (p. 187) has brown legs. The breeding Spotted Sandpiper (p. 151) has black spots on its chest.

**Stan's Notes:** Often seen in small flocks, combing shorelines and mudflats in search of food. Usually walks with its head down and tail up, ready to snatch up prey. Uses its long, straight bill to pluck insects and tiny fish out of the water. A member of the sandpiper group known as Tattlers, which scream alarm calls when taking off. Quite often moves into the water before taking flight, and gives a variety of flight notes at takeoff. Nest is a simple depression atop a mound of earth. Nests in marshes in the spruce forests of central Alaska and Canada. Migrates earlier than the Greater Yellowlegs in the fall and later in the spring.

**Long-billed Dowitcher**

breeding

winter
p. 267

# Short-billed Dowitcher
*Limnodromus griseus*

YEAR-ROUND
MIGRATION

**Size:** 11" (28 cm)

**Male:** Breeding plumage is an overall rusty brown with heavy black spots throughout. Has a small amount of white very low on belly. A long, straight black bill. Off-white eyebrow stripe. Dull yellow-to-green legs and feet.

**Female:** same as male

**Juvenile:** similar to winter adult

**Nest:** ground; female and male construct; 1 brood per year

**Eggs:** 3–4; olive-green with dark markings

**Incubation:** 20–21 days; male and female incubate

**Fledging:** 25–27 days; male and female feed the young

**Migration:** complete to non-migrator in Florida

**Food:** insects, snails, worms, leeches, seeds

**Compare:** Marbled Godwit (p. 199) is larger and has a two-toned, upturned bill and gray legs. Breeding Willet (p. 187) is larger, has a shorter bill and bold black-and-white wing linings, as seen in flight.

**Stan's Notes:** A common year-round resident found along coastal Florida and inland on freshwater lakes and marshes. With a rapid probing action like a sewing machine, it uses its long straight bill to probe deep into sand and mud for insects. Can be seen with the less common Long-billed Dowitcher (see inset), but it is difficult to tell the two apart.

# Killdeer
*Charadrius vociferus*

YEAR-ROUND

**Size:** 11" (28 cm)

**Male:** Upland shorebird with 2 black bands around the neck, like a necklace. Brown back and white belly. Bright reddish-orange rump, visible in flight.

**Female:** same as male

**Juvenile:** similar to adults, with a single neck band

**Nest:** ground; male scrapes; 2 broods per year

**Eggs:** 3–5; tan with brown markings

**Incubation:** 24–28 days; male and female incubate

**Fledging:** 25 days; male and female lead their young to food

**Migration:** non-migrator in Florida

**Food:** insects, worms, snails

**Compare:** The Spotted Sandpiper (p. 151) is found around water and lacks the 2 neck bands of the Killdeer. Semipalmated Plover (p. 239) shares the brown back and white belly, but is smaller and has a single black necklace.

**Stan's Notes:** Technically classified as a shorebird but lives in dry habitats instead of the shore. Often found in vacant fields, gravel pits, driveways, wetland edges or along railroad tracks. The only shorebird that has two black neck bands. Known to fake a broken wing to draw intruders away from the nest; once the nest is safe, the parent will take flight. Nests are just a slight depression in a dry area and are often hard to see. Hatchlings look like miniature adults walking on stilts. Soon after hatching, the young follow their parents around and peck for insects. Gives a loud and distinctive "kill-deer" call. Migrates in small flocks.

YEAR-ROUND

# Brown Thrasher
*Toxostoma rufum*

**Size:** 11" (28 cm)

**Male:** Rust-red with a long tail. Heavy streaking on the breast and belly. Two white wing bars. Long, curved bill and bright-yellow eyes.

**Female:** same as male

**Juvenile:** same as adults but with grayish eyes

**Nest:** cup; female and male build; 2 broods per year

**Eggs:** 4–5; pale blue with brown markings

**Incubation:** 11–14 days; female and male incubate

**Fledging:** 10–13 days; female and male feed the young

**Migration:** non-migrator in Florida

**Food:** insects, fruit

**Compare:** Slightly larger in size and similar in shape to the American Robin (p. 261) and Gray Catbird (p. 257), but the Brown Thrasher has a streaked chest, rusty color and yellow eyes. Look for the long rusty-red tail to help identify the Brown Thrasher.

**Stan's Notes:** A prodigious songster. Sings along forest edges and in suburban yards. Often found in thick shrubs, where it will sing deliberate musical phrases, repeating each twice. The male Brown Thrasher has the largest documented repertoire of all North American songbirds, with more than 1,100 types of songs. Builds nest low in dense shrubs, often in fencerows. Quickly flies or runs on the ground in and out of thick shrubs. A noisy feeder due to its habit of turning over leaves, small rocks and branches to find food. Seen year-round in Florida. Populations increase during winter months with the influx of northern birds.

male

female

YEAR-ROUND

# Northern Flicker
*Colaptes auratus*

**Size:** 12" (30 cm)

**Male:** Brown and black with a black mustache and black necklace. Red spot on the nape of the neck. Speckled chest. Large white rump patch, seen only when flying.

**Female:** same as male but without a black mustache

**Juvenile:** same as adult of the same sex

**Nest:** cavity; female and male excavate; 1 brood per year

**Eggs:** 5–8; white without markings

**Incubation:** 11–14 days; female and male incubate

**Fledging:** 25–28 days; female and male feed the young

**Migration:** non-migrator in Florida

**Food:** insects (especially ants and beetles); comes to suet feeders

**Compare:** The male Yellow-bellied Sapsucker (p. 57) has a red chin. The male Red-bellied Woodpecker (p. 63) has a red crown. Flickers are the only brown-backed woodpeckers in Florida.

**Stan's Notes:** This is the only woodpecker to regularly feed on the ground. Prefers ants and beetles and produces an antacid saliva that neutralizes the acidic defense of ants. The male often picks the nest site. Parents take up to 12 days to excavate the cavity. Can be attracted to your yard with a nest box stuffed with sawdust. Often reuses an old nest. Undulates deeply during flight, flashing yellow under its wings and tail and calling "wacka-wacka" loudly. Populations swell in winter with northern migrants.

# Mourning Dove
*Zenaida macroura*

**YEAR-ROUND**

**Size:** 12" (30 cm)

**Male:** Smooth and fawn-colored. Gray patch on the head. Iridescent pink and greenish blue on the neck. Black spot behind and below the eyes. Black spots on the wings and tail. Pointed, wedged tail; white edges seen in flight.

**Female:** similar to male, but lacks the pink-and-green iridescent neck feathers

**Juvenile:** spotted and streaked plumage

**Nest:** platform; female and male build; 2 broods per year

**Eggs:** 2; white without markings

**Incubation:** 13–14 days; male incubates during the day, female incubates at night

**Fledging:** 12–14 days; female and male feed the young

**Migration:** non-migrator in Florida

**Food:** seeds; will visit seed and ground feeders

**Compare:** Lacks the wide range of color combinations of the Rock Pigeon (p. 275). Lacks the black collar of the Eurasian Collared-Dove (p. 273).

**Stan's Notes:** Name comes from its mournful cooing. A ground feeder, bobbing its head as it walks. One of the few birds to drink without lifting its head, like the Rock Pigeon. The parents feed the young (squab) a regurgitated liquid called crop-milk during their first few days of life. Platform nest is so flimsy it often falls apart in a storm. During takeoff and in flight, wind rushes through the bird's wing feathers, creating a characteristic whistling sound.

winter

breeding

YEAR-ROUND

# Pied-billed Grebe
*Podilymbus podiceps*

**Size:** 12–14" (30–36 cm)

**Male:** Small and brown with a black chin and fluffy white patch beneath the tail. Black ring around a thick, chicken-like, ivory bill. Winter bill is brown and unmarked.

**Female:** same as male

**Juvenile:** paler than adults, with white spots and a gray chest, belly and bill

**Nest:** floating platform; female and male build; 1 brood per year

**Eggs:** 5–7; bluish white without markings

**Incubation:** 22–24 days; female and male incubate

**Fledging:** 45–60 days; female and male feed the young

**Migration:** non-migrator in Florida

**Food:** crayfish, aquatic insects, fish

**Compare:** Look for a puffy white patch under the tail and thick, chicken-like bill to help identify.

**Stan's Notes:** A common resident water bird, often seen diving for food. When disturbed, it slowly sinks like a submarine, quickly compressing its feathers, forcing the air out. Was called Hell-diver due to the length of time it can stay submerged. Able to surface far from where it went under. Well suited to life on water, with short wings, lobed toes, and legs set close to the rear of its body. Swims easily but moves awkwardly on land. Very sensitive to pollution. Builds nest on a floating mat in water. "Grebe" may originate from the Breton word *krib*, meaning "crest," referring to the crested head plumes of many grebes, especially during breeding season.

WINTER

# Greater Yellowlegs
*Tringa melanoleuca*

**Size:** 13–15" (33–38 cm)

**Male:** Tall with a bulbous head and a long, thin, slightly upturned bill. Gray streaking on the chest. White belly. Long yellow legs.

**Female:** same as male

**Juvenile:** same as adults

**Nest:** ground; female builds; 1 brood per year

**Eggs:** 3–4; off-white with brown markings

**Incubation:** 22–23 days; female and male incubate

**Fledging:** 18–20 days; male and female feed the young

**Migration:** complete, to Florida, other southern states

**Food:** small fish, aquatic insects

**Compare:** Breeding Willet (p. 187) is slightly larger, with a shorter neck and larger head, and it lacks bright-yellow legs. The breeding Spotted Sandpiper (p. 151) has spots on its chest. Look for the long yellow legs and long bill to identify the Greater Yellowlegs.

**Stan's Notes:** A common shorebird that can be identified by the slightly upturned bill and long yellow legs, which enable it to wade in deep water. Often seen resting on one leg. Rushes forward through the water to feed, plowing its bill or swinging it from side to side, catching small fish and insects. A skittish bird, it is quick to give an alarm call, causing flocks to take flight. Typically moves into the water before taking flight. Gives a variety of "flight" notes at takeoff. Nests on the ground close to water on the northern tundra of Labrador and Newfoundland. Migrates earlier than Lesser Yellowlegs in spring and later in fall.

male
p. 37

female

# Boat-tailed Grackle
*Quiscalus major*

YEAR-ROUND

| | |
|---|---|
| **Size:** | 13–15" (33–38 cm), female<br>15–17" (38–43 cm), male |
| **Female:** | A golden-brown chest and head. Nearly black wings and tail. Female is non-iridescent. |
| **Male:** | iridescent blue-black bird with a very long tail and bright-yellow eyes |
| **Juvenile:** | similar to female |
| **Nest:** | cup; female builds; 2 broods per year |
| **Eggs:** | 2–4; pale greenish blue with brown marks |
| **Incubation:** | 13–15 days; female incubates |
| **Fledging:** | 12–15 days; female feeds the young |
| **Migration:** | non-migrator; moves around to find food |
| **Food:** | insects, berries, seeds, fish; visits feeders |
| **Compare:** | Fairly distinctive. Not confused with many other birds. Found only along the coast. |

**Stan's Notes:** A noisy bird of coastal saltwater and inland marshes, giving several harsh, high-pitched calls and several squeaks. Eats a wide variety of foods from grains to fish. Sometimes seen picking insects off the backs of cattle. Will also visit bird feeders. Makes a cup nest with mud or cow dung and grass. Nests in small colonies. Most nesting occurs from February through July and occasionally again from October to December. Boat-taileds north of Gainesville have bright-yellow eyes, but in the rest of the state the birds have dark eyes. More common in Florida than the Common Grackle although less widespread.

breeding

winter
p. 277

displaying

# Willet

*Catoptrophorus semipalmatus*

YEAR-ROUND
WINTER

**Size:** 14–16" (36–40 cm)

**Male:** Brown breeding plumage with a white belly. Brown bill and legs. Distinctive black-and-white wing lining pattern, seen in flight or during display.

**Female:** same as male

**Juvenile:** similar to breeding adult, more tan in color

**Nest:** ground; female builds; 1 brood per year

**Eggs:** 3–5; olive-green with dark markings

**Incubation:** 24–28 days; male and female incubate

**Fledging:** 1–2 days; female and male feed young

**Migration:** non-migrator to complete in coastal Florida

**Food:** insects, small fish, crabs, worms, clams

**Compare:** Greater Yellowlegs (p. 183) is slightly smaller and has a smaller head, longer neck and yellow legs. Lesser Yellowlegs (p. 169) has yellow legs. The Marbled Godwit (p. 199) has a two-toned, upturned bill. Breeding Short-billed Dowitcher (p. 171) has yellow-greenish legs.

**Stan's Notes:** Common along coastal Florida during winter, with many continuing to migrate along the coast to the coast of South America. It appears a rich, warm brown during the breeding season and rather plain gray during the winter, but it always has a striking black-and-white wing pattern when seen in flight. Uses its black-and-white wing patches to display to its mate. Named after the "pill-will-willet" call it gives during the breeding season. Gives a "kip-kip-kip" alarm call when it takes flight. Nests along the Gulf and East Coasts, in some western states and Canada.

male

female

# Blue-winged Teal
*Spatula discors*

WINTER

**Size:** 15–16" (38–41 cm)

**Male:** Small, plain-looking brown duck with black speckles and a large, crescent-shaped white mark at the base of the bill. Gray head. Black tail with a small white patch. Blue wing patch (speculum), best seen in flight.

**Female:** duller than male, with only slight white at the base of the bill; lacks a crescent mark on the face and a white patch on the tail

**Juvenile:** same as female

**Nest:** ground; female builds; 1 brood per year

**Eggs:** 8–11; creamy white

**Incubation:** 23–27 days; female incubates

**Fledging:** 35–44 days; female feeds the young

**Migration:** complete, to Florida, other southern states

**Food:** aquatic plants, seeds, aquatic insects

**Compare:** The female Mallard (p. 209) has an orange-and-black bill. The female Wood Duck (p. 203) has a crest. Look for the white facial mark to identify the male Blue-winged.

**Stan's Notes:** One of the smallest ducks in North America and one of the longest-distance migrating ducks, with widespread nesting as far north as Alaska. One of the most widespread and abundant winter ducks in Florida. Arrives in August, leaves in April and May. Constructs its nest some distance from the water. Female performs a distraction display to protect nest and young. Male leaves female near the end of incubation. Planting crops and cultivating to pond edges have caused a decline in population.

soaring

# Red-shouldered Hawk

*Buteo lineatus*

YEAR-ROUND

| | |
|---|---|
| **Size:** | 15–19" (38–48 cm); up to 3½' wingspan |
| **Male:** | Reddish (cinnamon) head, shoulders, breast and belly. Wings and back are dark brown with white spots. Long tail with thin white bands and wide black bands. Obvious red wing linings, seen in flight. |
| **Female:** | same as male |
| **Juvenile:** | similar to adults but lacks the cinnamon color; white chest with dark spots |
| **Nest:** | platform; female and male build; 1 brood per year |
| **Eggs:** | 2–4; white with dark markings |
| **Incubation:** | 27–29 days; female and male incubate |
| **Fledging:** | 39–45 days; female and male feed the young |
| **Migration:** | non-migrator to partial migrator |
| **Food:** | reptiles, amphibians, large insects, birds |
| **Compare:** | The Red-tailed Hawk (p. 213) has a white chest. The Sharp-shinned Hawk (p. 271) is smaller and lacks the reddish head and belly of the Red-shouldered Hawk. |

**Stan's Notes:** A common woodland hawk in Florida, seen in backyards. Likes to hunt at forest edges, spotting snakes, frogs, insects, occasional small birds and other prey as it perches. Often flaps with an alternating gliding pattern. Very vocal with a distinct scream. Breeds when it reaches 2–3 years. Remains in the same territory for many years. Starts constructing its nest in February. Young leave the nest by June.

female

male
p. 71

# Hooded Merganser
*Lophodytes cucullatus*

WINTER

**Size:** 16–19" (41–48 cm)

**Female:** Sleek brown-and-rust bird with a red head. Ragged "hair" on the back of the head. Long, thin, brown bill.

**Male:** black back, rust-brown sides, long black bill; raises crest "hood" to display a white patch

**Juvenile:** similar to female

**Nest:** cavity; female lines an old woodpecker cavity or a nest box near water; 1 brood per year

**Eggs:** 10–12; white without markings

**Incubation:** 32–33 days; female incubates

**Fledging:** 71 days; female feeds the young

**Migration:** complete to non-migrator in Florida

**Food:** small fish, aquatic insects, crustaceans (especially crayfish)

**Compare:** Look for the ragged "hair" on the back of the head of the female Hoodie.

**Stan's Notes:** A small diving duck, found in shallow ponds, sloughs, lakes and rivers. Usually in small groups. Quick, low flight across the water, with fast wingbeats. Male has a deep, rolling call. Female gives a hoarse quack. Nests in wooded areas. Female will lay some eggs in the nests of other mergansers or Wood Ducks (egg dumping), resulting in 20–25 eggs in some nests. Rarely, she shares a nest, sitting with a Wood Duck.

male p. 73

female

WINTER

# Ring-necked Duck
*Aythya collaris*

**Size:** 16–19" (41–48 cm)

**Female:** Brown with a darker brown back and crown and lighter-brown sides. Gray face. White eye-ring with a white line behind the eye. White ring around the bill. Peaked head.

**Male:** black head, chest and back; gray-to-white sides; blue bill with a bold white ring and a thinner ring at the base; peaked head

**Juvenile:** similar to female

**Nest:** ground; female builds; 1 brood per year

**Eggs:** 8–10; olive to brown without markings

**Incubation:** 26–27 days; female incubates

**Fledging:** 49–56 days; female teaches the young to feed

**Migration:** complete, to Florida, other southern states

**Food:** aquatic plants and insects

**Compare:** Look for the white ring around the bill to help identify the female Ring-necked Duck.

**Stan's Notes:** One of the most abundant wintering ducks in the state. Often seen in larger freshwater lakes, usually in small flocks or just pairs. A diving duck, watch for it to dive underwater to forage for food. Springs up off the water to take flight. Has a distinctive tall, peaked head with a sloped forehead. Flattens its crown when diving. Male gives a quick series of grating barks and grunts. Female gives high-pitched peeps. Named "Ring-necked" for its cinnamon collar, which is nearly impossible to see in the field. Also called Ring-billed Duck due to the white ring on its bill.

in flight

male
p. 281

female

juvenile

juvenile
in flight

# Snail Kite

*Rostrhamus sociabilis*

YEAR-ROUND

**Size:** 17–19" (43–48 cm); up to 3¾' wingspan

**Female:** Dark brown with small white patches. White face and chin. Hooked bill. Bold yellow patch at the base of the bill. Light-orange legs and feet.

**Male:** dark-gray bird with black tail and wing tips, white rump and undertail, red eyes and orange legs and feet

**Juvenile:** similar to female; bill is shorter and less hooked than adult bill

**Nest:** platform; male builds; 1 brood per year

**Eggs:** 2–4; white with brown markings

**Incubation:** 26–30 days; female and male incubate

**Fledging:** 23–28 days; male and female feed the young

**Migration:** non-migrator; moves to find food in winter

**Food:** apple snails, turtles

**Compare:** Swallow-tailed Kite (p. 87) has a forked tail and white head and chest. Snail Kite is a habitat specialist and is not seen away from bodies of water.

**Stan's Notes:** Once known as the Everglade Kite. Not very common, with populations restricted to wet habitats that have ample snails. Feeds mostly on the large apple snail. Will take advantage of times of high water levels, when more snails are available. Quickly and easily extricates the entire snail from the shell before swallowing it whole. Litter piles of empty snail shells accumulate below a favorite feeding perch. Also feeds on turtles. Uses its long curved bill to reach inside the turtle shell and extract meat a little bit at a time. A highly managed bird in Florida and considered endangered.

# Marbled Godwit
*Limosa fedoa*

MIGRATION
WINTER

**Size:** 18" (45 cm)

**Male:** Tawny brown overall with a darker back. Long, two-toned and slightly upturned bill with black tip and pinkish base. Long gray legs. Cinnamon under wings, seen in flight.

**Female:** same as male

**Juvenile:** similar to adult

**Nest:** ground; female and male construct; 1 brood per year

**Eggs:** 3–5; olive-green with dark markings

**Incubation:** 21–23 days; male and female incubate

**Fledging:** 20–21 days; female and male feed the young

**Migration:** complete, to coastal Florida

**Food:** aquatic insects, snails, worms, leeches

**Compare:** Breeding Willet (p. 187) is smaller. Whimbrel (p. 201) is the same size and has a down-curved bill, compared with the slightly upturned bill of the Godwit. Breeding Short-billed Dowitcher (p. 171) is smaller and more common and has a straight black bill.

**Stan's Notes:** A winter resident that is easily identified by its very long, two-toned, slightly upturned bill. Uses its bill to probe deep into sand and mud for insects. Usually feeds in mid-thigh water. In the winter, prefers saltwater beaches and mud flats up and down the East Coast. Returns to Prairie Pothole regions of North Dakota and Canada where it nests in shortgrass prairie near wetlands. Name comes from its "god*whit*-god*whit*" call.

# Whimbrel

*Numenius phaeopus*

MIGRATION
WINTER

**Size:** 18" (45 cm)

**Male:** Heavily streaked bird, light brown to gray. A long down-curved bill and multiple dark brown stripes on crown. Dark line through eyes. Legs are light gray to blue.

**Female:** same as male

**Juvenile:** similar to adult

**Nest:** ground; female and male construct; 1 brood per year

**Eggs:** 3–4; olive-green with dark markings

**Incubation:** 27–28 days; male and female incubate

**Fledging:** 35–42 days; female and male feed the young

**Migration:** complete, to coastal Florida

**Food:** insects, snails, worms, leeches, berries

**Compare:** The breeding Willet (p. 187) lacks a crown with brown stripes and long down-curved bill. Marbled Godwit (p. 199) is the same size and has an upturned bill. Short-billed Dowitcher (p. 171) is more common and has a straight black bill. Greater Yellowlegs (p. 183) is smaller and has yellow legs.

**Stan's Notes:** A winter resident, easily identified by its very long down-curved bill and brown stripes on head. Uses its bill to probe deep into sand and mud for insects. Unlike the other shorebirds, berries become an important food source in summer. Is very vocal, giving single note whistles. Returns to tundra of northern Alaska to nest. Doesn't breed until age 3. Has a long-term pair bond. Adults leave breeding grounds up to two weeks before the young leave.

male
p. 301

female

# Wood Duck
*Aix sponsa*

YEAR-ROUND
WINTER

**Size:** 17–20" (43–51 cm)

**Female:** Small brown dabbling duck. Bright-white eye-ring and a not-so-obvious crest. Blue patch on wings (speculum), often hidden.

**Male:** highly ornamented, with a mostly green head and crest patterned with black and white; rusty chest, white belly and red eyes

**Juvenile:** similar to female

**Nest:** cavity; female lines an old woodpecker cavity or a nest box in a tree; 1 brood per year

**Eggs:** 10–15; creamy white without markings

**Incubation:** 28–36 days; female incubates

**Fledging:** 56–68 days; female teaches the young to feed

**Migration:** non-migrator to partial in Florida

**Food:** aquatic insects, plants, seeds

**Compare:** The female Mallard (p. 209) and female Blue-winged Teal (p. 189) lack the eye-ring and crest. The female Northern Shoveler (p. 207) is larger and has a large spoon-shaped bill.

**Stan's Notes:** A common duck of quiet, shallow backwater ponds. Nearly went extinct around 1900 due to overhunting, but it's doing well now. Nests in a tree cavity or a nest box in a tree. Seen flying in forests or perching on high branches. Female takes off with a loud, squealing call and enters the nest cavity from full flight. Lays some eggs in a neighboring nest (egg dumping), resulting in more than 20 eggs in some clutches. Hatchlings stay in the nest for 24 hours, then jump from as high as 60 feet (18 m) to the ground or water to follow their mother. They never return to the nest.

male

female

WINTER

# American Wigeon
*Mareca americana*

**Size:** 18–20" (48 cm)

**Male:** Brown duck with a rounded head and obvious white cap. Deep-green patch starting behind the eyes and streaking down the neck. Long pointed tail. Short, black-tipped grayish bill. White belly and wing linings, seen in flight. Non-breeding lacks white cap and green patch.

**Female:** light brown with a pale gray head, a short, black-tipped grayish bill, green wing patch (speculum) and dark eye spot; white belly and wing linings, seen in flight

**Juvenile:** similar to female

**Nest:** ground; female builds; 1 brood per year

**Eggs:** 7–12; white without markings

**Incubation:** 23–25 days; female incubates

**Fledging:** 37–48 days; female teaches the young to feed

**Migration:** complete, to Florida, other southern states

**Food:** aquatic plants, seeds

**Compare:** Male American Wigeon is easily identified by the white cap and black-tipped grayish bill. Look for the black-tipped grayish bill and green wing patch to help identify the female American Wigeon.

**Stan's Notes:** Often in small flocks or with other ducks. Prefers shallow lakes. Male stays with the female only during the first week of incubation. Female raises the young. If threatened, female feigns injury while the young run and hide. Conceals upland nest in tall vegetation within 50–250 yards (46–229 m) of water.

male p. 307

female

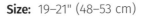

# Northern Shoveler
*Anas clypeata*

WINTER

**Size:** 19–21" (48–53 cm)

**Female:** A medium-sized brown duck speckled with black. Green patch on the wings (speculum). An extraordinarily large, spoon-shaped bill.

**Male:** iridescent green head, rusty sides, white chest and a large spoon-shaped bill

**Juvenile:** same as female

**Nest:** ground; female builds; 1 brood per year

**Eggs:** 9–12; olive without markings

**Incubation:** 22–25 days; female incubates

**Fledging:** 30–60 days; female leads the young to food

**Migration:** complete, to Florida, other southern states, Mexico and Central America

**Food:** aquatic insects, plants

**Compare:** The female Wood Duck (p. 203) is smaller and has a white eye-ring. The female Mallard (p. 209) lacks the large bill. Look for the spoon-shaped bill to identify the Shoveler.

**Stan's Notes:** One of several species of shovelers. Called "Shoveler" due to the peculiar, shovel-like shape of its bill. Given the common name "Northern" because it is the only species of these ducks in North America. Seen in shallow wetlands, ponds and small lakes in flocks of 5–10 birds. Flocks fly in tight formation. Swims low in water, pointing its large bill toward the water as if it's too heavy to lift. Usually swims in tight circles while feeding. Feeds mainly by filtering tiny aquatic insects and plants from the surface of the water with its bill. Female gathers plant material and forms it into a nest a short distance from the water. This winter visitor arrives in Florida in September and leaves in April.

male
p. 305

female

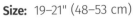

# Mallard
*Anas platyrhynchos*

**YEAR-ROUND**

| | |
|---|---|
| **Size:** | 19–21" (48–53 cm) |
| **Female:** | Brown duck with a blue-and-white wing mark (speculum). Orange-and-black bill. |
| **Male:** | large green head, white necklace, rust-brown or chestnut chest, combination of gray-and-white sides, yellow bill, orange legs and feet |
| **Juvenile:** | same as female but with a yellow bill |
| **Nest:** | ground; female builds; 1 brood per year |
| **Eggs:** | 7–10; greenish to whitish, unmarked |
| **Incubation:** | 26–30 days; female incubates |
| **Fledging:** | 42–52 days; female leads the young to food |
| **Migration:** | non-migrator in Florida |
| **Food:** | seeds, plants, aquatic insects; will come to ground feeders offering corn |
| **Compare:** | The female Wood Duck (p. 203) has a white eye-ring. The female Blue-winged Teal (p. 189) is smaller than the female Mallard. |

**Stan's Notes:** A familiar dabbling duck of lakes and ponds. Also found in rivers, streams and some backyards. Tips forward to feed on vegetation on the bottom of shallow water. The name "Mallard" comes from the Latin word *masculus,* meaning "male," referring to the male's habit of taking no part in raising the young. Female and male have white underwings and white tails, but only the male has black central tail feathers that curl upward. The female gives a classic quack. Returns to its birthplace each year.

male
p. 285

female

soaring

# Northern Harrier
*Circus hudsonius*

WINTER

**Size:** 18–22" (45–56 cm); up to 4' wingspan

**Female:** Slender, low-flying hawk with a dark-brown back and brown streaking on the chest and belly. Large white rump patch. Thin black tail bands and black wing tips. Yellow eyes.

**Male:** silver-gray with a large white rump patch and white belly; faint, thin bands across tail, black wing tips and yellow eyes

**Juvenile:** similar to female, with an orange breast

**Nest:** ground; female and male construct; 1 brood per year

**Eggs:** 4–8; bluish white without markings

**Incubation:** 31–32 days; female incubates

**Fledging:** 30–35 days; male and female feed the young

**Migration:** complete, to Florida, other southern states, Mexico and Central America

**Food:** mice, snakes, insects, small birds

**Compare:** Slimmer than the Red-tailed Hawk (p. 213). Look for the characteristic low gliding and the black tail bands to identify the female Harrier.

**Stan's Notes:** One of the easiest of hawks to identify. Glides just above the ground, following the contours of the land while searching for prey. Holds its wings just above horizontal, tilting back and forth in the wind, similar to the Turkey Vulture. Formerly called Marsh Hawk due to its habit of hunting over marshes. Feeds and nests on the ground. Will also preen and rest on the ground. Unlike other hawks, mainly uses its hearing to find prey, followed by its sight. At any age, it has a distinctive owl-like face disk.

soaring

juvenile
soaring

juvenile

# Red-tailed Hawk
*Buteo jamaicensis*

YEAR-ROUND
WINTER

**Size:** 19–23" (48–58 cm); up to 4½' wingspan

**Male:** Variety of colorations, from chocolate brown to nearly all white. Often brown with a white breast and brown belly band. Rust-red tail. Underside of wing is white with a small dark patch on the leading edge near the shoulder.

**Female:** same as male but slightly larger

**Juvenile:** similar to adults, with a speckled breast and light eyes; lacks a red tail

**Nest:** platform; male and female build; 1 brood per year

**Eggs:** 2–3; white without markings or sometimes marked with brown

**Incubation:** 30–35 days; female and male incubate

**Fledging:** 45–46 days; male and female feed the young

**Migration:** non-migrator to partial migrator

**Food:** small and medium-size animals, large birds, snakes, fish, insects, bats, carrion

**Compare:** Red-shouldered Hawk (p. 191) and Sharp-shinned Hawk (p. 271) are much smaller.

**Stan's Notes:** Common in open country and cities. Seen perching on fences, freeway lampposts and trees. Look for it circling above open fields and roadsides, searching for prey. Gives a high-pitched scream that trails off. Often builds a large stick nest in large trees along roads. Lines nest with finer material, like evergreen needles. Returns to the same nest site each year. The red tail develops in the second year and is best seen from above.

YEAR-ROUND

# Barred Owl
*Strix varia*

| | |
|---|---|
| **Size:** | 20–24" (51–61 cm); up to 3½' wingspan |
| **Male:** | Chunky brown-and-gray owl. Dark horizontal barring on upper chest. Vertical streaks on lower chest and belly. A large head and dark-brown eyes. Yellow bill and feet. |
| **Female:** | same as male but slightly larger |
| **Juvenile:** | light gray with a black face |
| **Nest:** | cavity; does not add any nesting material; 1 brood per year |
| **Eggs:** | 2–3; white without markings |
| **Incubation:** | 28–33 days; female incubates |
| **Fledging:** | 42–44 days; female and male feed the young |
| **Migration:** | non-migrator |
| **Food:** | mice, rabbits and other animals; small birds; fish; reptiles; amphibians |
| **Compare:** | Great Horned Owl (p. 219) has "horns," and the much smaller Eastern Screech-Owl (p. 255) has ears, both of which the Barred Owl lacks. Burrowing Owl (p. 163) has long legs and is less than half the size of the Barred Owl. Look for a stocky owl with a large head and dark-brown eyes to identify the Barred Owl. |

**Stan's Notes:** Prefers deciduous woodlands but can be attracted to your yard with a simple nest box that has a large entrance hole. Often seen hunting during the day. Perches and watches for mice, birds and other prey. Hovers over water and reaches down to grab fish. After fledging, the young stay with the parents for up to four months. Often sounds like a dog barking before calling six to eight hoots, sounding like "who-who-who-cooks-for-you."

YEAR-ROUND

# Mottled Duck
*Anas fulvigula*

| | |
|---|---|
| **Size:** | 21–23" (53-58 cm) |
| **Male:** | All-brown duck with a light-tan neck and head. Bright-yellow bill without markings. Wing patch (speculum) is blue (sometimes green) and outlined with black. |
| **Female:** | same as male |
| **Juvenile:** | same as adult |
| **Nest:** | ground; female builds; 1 brood per year |
| **Eggs:** | 5–10; off-white without markings |
| **Incubation:** | 25–27 days; female incubates |
| **Fledging:** | 60–70 days; female shows young what to eat |
| **Migration:** | non-migrator in Florida |
| **Food:** | aquatic insects, crayfish, snails, grass, seeds |
| **Compare:** | Female Mallard (p. 209) has an orange bill with black markings, and its speculum is outlined with white. Look for the female Mottled Duck's black-outlined speculum. |

**Stan's Notes:** A year-round resident and widely hunted in Florida. It is most densely populated around the coast in both freshwater and saltwater marshes. Feeds on more insects and crayfish than the Mallard. Will breed with Mallards, producing hybrids. Mated pairs stay together all year, unlike Mallards. Young will scatter if mother feels threatened and gives an alarm call.

# Great Horned Owl
*Bubo virginianus*

YEAR-ROUND

**Size:** 21–25" (53–64 cm); up to 4' wingspan

**Male:** Robust brown "horned" owl. Bright-yellow eyes and a V-shaped white throat resembling a necklace. Horizontal barring on the chest.

**Female:** same as male but slightly larger

**Juvenile:** similar to adults but lacks ear tufts

**Nest:** no nest; takes over the nest of a crow, hawk or Great Blue Heron or uses a partial cavity, stump or broken tree; 1 brood per year

**Eggs:** 2–3; white without markings

**Incubation:** 26–30 days; female incubates

**Fledging:** 30–35 days; male and female feed the young

**Migration:** non-migrator

**Food:** mammals, birds (ducks), snakes, insects

**Compare:** Burrowing Owl (p. 163) is much smaller and has long legs. Barred Owl (p. 215) has dark eyes and no "horns." The Eastern Screech-Owl (p. 255) is extremely tiny. Look for bright-yellow eyes and feather "horns" on the head to help identify the Great Horned Owl.

**Stan's Notes:** The largest owl and a winter nester in Florida, laying eggs in January and February. Able to hunt in complete darkness due to its excellent hearing. The "horns," or "ears," are tufts of feathers and have nothing to do with hearing. Cannot turn its head all the way around. Wing feathers are ragged on the ends, resulting in silent flight. Eyelids close from the top down, like humans. Fearless, it is one of the few animals that will kill skunks and porcupines. Given that, it is also called the Flying Tiger. Call sounds like "hoo-hoo-hoo-hoooo."

breeding

winter

# Glossy Ibis
*Plegadis falcinellus*

**Size:** 22–24" (56-60 cm); up to 3' wingspan

**Male:** Breeding male has a chestnut brown head and neck. Iridescent green and blue wings and tail. Appears to be all dark brown from a distance. Very long, down-curved bill with blue facial skin near base. Winter is overall dark with a speckled head.

**Female:** same as male

**Juvenile:** same as adult, but lacks iridescent coloring

**Nest:** platform; female and male build; 1 brood per year

**Eggs:** 2–4; light blue without markings

**Incubation:** 20–21 days; female and male incubate

**Fledging:** 28–32 days; female and male feed the young

**Migration:** partial to non-migrator in Florida

**Food:** aquatic insects, crustaceans

**Compare:** One of two ibis species in Florida, the long, down-curved bill helps identify them. White Ibis (p. 343) is all white and not confused with the brown Glossy Ibis.

**Stan's Notes:** One of two native ibis species in Florida. Seems to be on the increase in the state. Prefers fresh water over salt water, with crayfish a big part of the diet. From a distance the bird appears dark brown or nearly black, but when seen up close or through binoculars its iridescent green and bluish purple colors are amazing. Its long down-curved bill helps identify it in flight. Often seen flying in groups of 30 or more. Nests in large colonies with other wading birds.

displaying
male

non-
displaying

female

# Wild Turkey
*Meleagris gallopavo*

YEAR-ROUND

**Size:** 36–48" (91–122 cm)

**Male:** Large brown-and-bronze bird with a naked blue-and-red head. Long, straight, black beard in the center of the chest. Tail spreads open like a fan. Spurs on legs.

**Female:** thinner and less striking than the male; often lacks a breast beard

**Juvenile:** same as adult of the same sex

**Nest:** ground; female builds; 1 brood per year

**Eggs:** 10–12; buff-white with dull-brown markings

**Incubation:** 27–28 days; female incubates

**Fledging:** 6–10 days; female leads the young to food

**Migration:** non-migrator; moves around to find food

**Food:** insects, seeds, fruit

**Compare:** This bird is quite distinctive and unlikely to be confused with others.

**Stan's Notes:** The largest native game bird in Florida, and the species from which the domestic turkey was bred. A strong flier that can approach 60 mph (97 kph). Can fly straight up, then away. Eyesight is three times better than ours. Hearing is also excellent; can hear competing males up to a mile away. Male has a "harem" of up to 20 females. Female scrapes out a shallow depression for nesting and pads it with soft leaves. Males are known as toms, females are hens, and young are poults. Roosts in trees at night. Eliminated from many of the eastern states by the turn of the 20th century due to market hunting and loss of habitat, and reintroduced in the 1960–80s. Populations are now stable.

juvenile

breeding

non-breeding

chick-feeding
adult

# Brown Pelican
*Pelecanus occidentalis*

YEAR-ROUND

**Size:** 46–50" (117–127 cm); up to 7' wingspan

**Male:** Gray-brown body, black belly, exceptionally long gray bill. Breeding adult has a white or yellow head with dark chestnut hind neck. Adult that is feeding chicks (chick-feeding adult) has a speckled white head. A non-breeding adult has a white head and neck.

**Female:** similar to male

**Juvenile:** brown with white breast and belly; does not acquire adult plumage until the third year

**Nest:** ground; female and male build; 1 brood per year

**Eggs:** 2–4; white without markings

**Incubation:** 28–30 days; female and male incubate

**Fledging:** 71–86 days; female and male feed the young

**Migration:** non-migrator along coastal Florida

**Food:** fish

**Compare:** A large, unmistakable bird in Florida

**Stan's Notes:** Common bird of Florida now, although it was recently an endangered species. Suffering from eggshell thinning in the 1970s due to DDT and other pesticides, it is now reestablishing along the East, Gulf and West Coasts. Captures fish by diving headfirst into the ocean, opening its large bill and "netting" fish with its gular pouch (an expandable membrane beneath its lower jaw). Often seen sitting on posts around marinas. Nests in large colonies. Doesn't breed before the age of 3, when it obtains its breeding plumage.

WINTER

# Ruby-crowned Kinglet
*Regulus calendula*

| | |
|---|---|
| **Size:** | 4" (10 cm) |
| **Male:** | Small, teardrop-shaped green-to-gray bird. Two white wing bars and a white eye-ring. Hidden ruby crown. |
| **Female:** | same as male, but lacks a ruby crown |
| **Juvenile:** | same as female |
| **Nest:** | pendulous; female builds; 1 brood per year |
| **Eggs:** | 4–5; white with brown markings |
| **Incubation:** | 11–12 days; female incubates |
| **Fledging:** | 11–12 days; female and male feed the young |
| **Migration:** | complete, to Florida, other southern states, Mexico and Central America |
| **Food:** | insects, berries |
| **Compare:** | The female American Goldfinch (p. 351) shares the drab olive plumage and unmarked chest, but it is larger. Look for the white eye-ring to identify the Ruby-crowned Kinglet. |

**Stan's Notes:** This is one of the smaller birds in Florida. Most commonly seen during migration. Look for it flitting around thick shrubs low to the ground. It takes a quick eye to see the ruby crown, which the male flashes when he is excited. The female weaves an unusually intricate nest and fastens colorful lichens and mosses to the exterior with spiderwebs. Often builds the nest high in a mature tree, where it hangs from a branch that has overlapping leaves. Sings a distinctive song that starts out soft and ends loud and on a higher note. "Kinglet" originates from the word *king*, referring to the male's red crown, and the diminutive suffix *let*, meaning "small."

# Brown-headed Nuthatch
*Sitta pusilla*

YEAR-ROUND

**Size:** 4½" (11 cm)

**Male:** Gray back and dull-white chin, breast and belly. Brown cap bordered by a black line that extends through eyes. Pale gray spot at the nape of neck, hard to see from a distance.

**Female:** same as male

**Juvenile:** same as adult

**Nest:** cavity; female and male construct; 1 brood per year

**Eggs:** 3–5; white with dark markings

**Incubation:** 12–14 days; female incubates

**Fledging:** 18–19 days; female and male feed the young

**Migration:** non-migrator

**Food:** insects, seeds; comes to seed feeders

**Compare:** Carolina Chickadee (p. 231) is similar in size, but it has a black cap. Look for the brown cap of the Brown-headed Nuthatch.

**Stan's Notes:** A tiny bird of open pine forest in Florida. Like other nuthatches, it feeds by creeping up and down twigs and trunks of trees, looking for insects and insect eggs. Works hard to remove seeds from cones on evergreen trees. Has been known to cache pine seeds for later consumption. Visits seed feeders. A cavity nester, it excavates a cavity, takes an abandoned woodpecker home or uses a nest box. Occasionally an unmated male helper attends to a mated female on the nest. Will stay with mate nearly all year, defending a very small territory.

# Carolina Chickadee
*Poecile carolinensis*

YEAR-ROUND

**Size:** 5" (13 cm)

**Male:** Mostly gray with a black cap and chin. White face and chest with a tan belly. Darker-gray tail.

**Female:** same as male

**Juvenile:** same as adult

**Nest:** cavity; female and male build or excavate; 1–2 broods per year

**Eggs:** 5–7; white with reddish brown markings

**Incubation:** 11–12 days; female and male incubate

**Fledging:** 13–17 days; female and male feed the young

**Migration:** non-migrator

**Food:** insects, seeds, fruit; comes to seed and suet feeders

**Compare:** Brown-headed Nuthatch (p. 229) is similar in size, but it lacks the black cap and chin. Tufted Titmouse (p. 235) is a close relative, but it has an erect crest and lacks the black cap and chin.

**Stan's Notes:** A common year-round bird of Florida. One of the first birds to use a newly placed feeder. Flies to a feeder, grabs a seed and carries it to a branch. To get to the meat inside, it holds the seed down with its feet and hammers the shell open with its bill. Returns for another seed. A friendly bird. Can be tamed and hand fed. Attracted with a nest box that has a 1¼-inch entrance hole. Female gives a loud snake-like hiss if disturbed on the nest. Often seen with other birds (mixed flock) in winter. Song is a high, fast "chika-dee-dee-dee-dee."

male

female

first
winter

# Yellow-rumped Warbler
*Setophaga coronata*

MIGRATION
WINTER

**Size:** 5–6" (13–15 cm)

**Male:** Slate gray with black streaking on the chest. Yellow patches on the head, flanks and rump. White chin and belly. Two white wing bars.

**Female:** duller gray than the male, mixed with brown

**Juvenile:** first winter is similar to the adult female

**Nest:** cup; female builds; 2 broods per year

**Eggs:** 4–5; white with brown markings

**Incubation:** 12–13 days; female incubates

**Fledging:** 10–12 days; female and male feed young

**Migration:** complete, to Florida, other southern states, Mexico and Central America

**Food:** insects, berries; visits suet feeders in spring

**Compare:** Male Common Yellowthroat (p. 353) has a yellow breast and a very distinctive black mask. The Palm Warbler (p. 357) has a yellow throat and chestnut cap. Look for a combination of yellow patches on the rump, flanks and head of Yellow-rumped Warbler.

**Stan's Notes:** This is one of our most common winter warblers. Migrates north to northern states and Canada in the spring. Familiar call is a single robust "chip," heard mostly during migration. Sings a wonderful song in spring. Comes to suet feeders in spring, when insect populations are low. Moves quickly among trees and from the ground to trees. Flits around the upper branches of tall trees. In the fall, the male molts to a dull color similar to the female, but he retains his yellow patches all year. Also called Myrtle Warbler. Sometimes called Butter-butt due to the yellow patch on its rump.

233

# Tufted Titmouse

*Baeolophus bicolor*

YEAR-ROUND

**Size:** 6" (15 cm)

**Male:** Slate gray with a white chest and belly. Pointed crest. Rust-brown wash on the flanks. Gray legs and dark eyes.

**Female:** same as male

**Juvenile:** same as adult

**Nest:** cavity; female lines an old woodpecker cavity; 2 broods per year

**Eggs:** 5–7; white with brown markings

**Incubation:** 13–14 days; female incubates

**Fledging:** 15–18 days; female and male feed the young

**Migration:** non-migrator

**Food:** insects, seeds, fruit; will come to seed and suet feeders

**Compare:** The Carolina Chickadee (p. 231) is a close relative but is smaller and lacks a crest. The Brown-headed Nuthatch (p. 229) is smaller. Look for the pointed crest to help identify the Tufted Titmouse.

**Stan's Notes:** A common feeder bird that can be attracted with an offering of black oil sunflower seeds or suet. Can also be attracted with a nest box. Well known for its "peter-peter-peter" call, which it quickly repeats. Notorious for pulling hair from sleeping dogs, cats and squirrels to line its nest. Usually seen only one or two at a time. Male feeds female during courtship and nesting. The prefix *tit* in the common name comes from a Scandinavian word meaning "little." Suffix *mouse* is derived from the Old English word *mase*, meaning "bird." Simply translated, it is a "small bird."

breeding
p. 139

winter

# Least Sandpiper
*Calidris minutilla*

MIGRATION
WINTER

**Size:** 6" (15 cm)

**Male:** Winter plumage is overall gray to light brown, with a distinct brown breast band and white belly. Light-gray eyebrows and short, thin, down-curved black bill. Dull-yellow legs.

**Female:** same as male

**Juvenile:** similar to winter adult, but buff-brown and lacks the breast band

**Nest:** ground; male and female construct; 1 brood per year

**Eggs:** 3–4; olive with dark markings

**Incubation:** 19–23 days; male and female incubate

**Fledging:** 25–28 days; male and female feed the young

**Migration:** complete, to coastal Florida

**Food:** aquatic and terrestrial insects, seeds

**Compare:** The smallest of sandpipers. Often confused with winter Western Sandpiper (p. 241) and Semipalmated Sandpiper (p. 239), Least Sandpiper's yellow legs differentiate it from other tiny sandpipers. Look for the short, thin, down-curved bill to help identify.

**Stan's Notes:** A winter resident in coastal Florida. Also winters in southern coastal states from the Carolinas to California. This is a tiny, tame sandpiper that can be approached without scaring it. It is the smallest of peeps (sandpipers), nesting on the tundra in northern regions of Canada and Alaska. Prefers the grassy flats of saltwater and freshwater ponds. Its yellow legs can be hard to see in water, poor light or when covered with mud. Most other small shorebirds have black legs and feet.

breeding

winter

# Semipalmated Sandpiper
*Calidris pusilla*

MIGRATION

**Size:** 6" (15 cm)

**Male:** Plump gray shorebird. Winter plumage has a grayish-brown head, neck and back and a white chest. White eyebrows and short, straight, blunt-tipped black bill. Black legs. Breeding plumage (usually seen in the Arctic) has a brown head, some black and brown spots on the back and a white belly.

**Female:** same as male

**Juvenile:** overall gray-brown with black spots

**Nest:** ground; male and female construct; 1 brood per year

**Eggs:** 2–4; light yellow with brown markings

**Incubation:** 18–22 days; male and female incubate

**Fledging:** 18–20 days; male and female feed the young

**Migration:** complete, to the Bahamas and northern South America

**Food:** aquatic insects

**Compare:** Winter Sanderling (p. 251) is much larger and lighter in color.

**Stan's Notes:** The most common shorebird in Florida, seen during spring migration (mid-May to early June) and autumn migration (July to August). Few individuals remain year-round. The male does most of the care of the young after hatching, since the female abandons her family approximately 2–3 days after the eggs hatch. Retains the same mate for several years. Nests in northern Canada and Alaska.

breeding
p. 141

winter

# Western Sandpiper
*Calidris mauri*

MIGRATION
WINTER

**Size:** 6½" (16 cm)

**Male:** Winter plumage is dull gray to light brown overall with a white belly and eyebrows. Black legs. Narrow bill that droops near tip.

**Female:** same as male

**Juvenile:** similar to breeding adult, bright buff-brown on the back only

**Nest:** ground; male and female construct; 1 brood per year

**Eggs:** 2–4; light brown with dark markings

**Incubation:** 20–22 days; male and female incubate

**Fledging:** 19–21 days; male and female feed the young

**Migration:** complete, to coastal Florida

**Food:** aquatic and terrestrial insects

**Compare:** Winter Least Sandpiper (p. 237) is similar, but lacks black legs. Semipalmated Sandpiper (p. 239) is also similar, but it has a blunt-tipped bill that doesn't droop. Look for black legs and a longer bill that droops slightly at the tip to identify the Western Sandpiper.

**Stan's Notes:** A coastal winter resident in southern states from the Carolinas to California. Nests on the ground in large "loose" colonies on the tundra of northern coastal Alaska. Adults leave their breeding grounds several weeks before the young. Some obtain their breeding plumage before leaving Florida in spring. Feeds on insects at the water's edge, sometimes immersing its head. Feeds in deeper water than the Semipalmated Sandpiper. Young leave the nest (precocial) within a few hours after hatching. Female leaves and the male tends the hatchlings.

# Common Ground-Dove
*Columbina passerina*

YEAR-ROUND

**Size:** 6½" (16 cm)

**Male:** A very small dove with a short tail and a unique scalloped appearance on head and chest. Black-tipped reddish orange bill and slate gray crown. Pinkish-gray underside. Bright chestnut wing linings, seen in flight.

**Female:** similar to male, but grayer and has a more uniform color

**Juvenile:** similar to adult

**Nest:** ground; female and male build; 2–4 broods per year

**Eggs:** 2–4; white without markings

**Incubation:** 12–14 days; female and male incubate

**Fledging:** 10–11 days; female and male feed young

**Migration:** non-migrator

**Food:** seeds, berries; will come to seed feeders

**Compare:** The Mourning Dove (p. 179) is twice the size of Common Ground-Dove and lacks the scalloped appearance and chestnut-colored wing linings.

**Stan's Notes:** The smallest dove in Florida, formerly called Eastern Ground Dove. Known to continually bob its head. Frequently seen in pairs. Unafraid of humans and spends most of its time on the ground. While it usually nests on the ground, it sometimes builds a flimsy nest in a shrub or takes an abandoned nest low in a tree. Seen in open dry woodlands, old fields and pastures. Walks around with mechanical movements, bobbing its head and shuffling its feet like a wind-up toy.

# Eastern Phoebe
*Sayornis phoebe*

WINTER

**Size:** 7" (18 cm)

**Male:** Plain gray with slightly darker wings, a light-olive belly and a thin, dark bill.

**Female:** same as male

**Juvenile:** same as adults

**Nest:** cup; female builds; 2 broods per year

**Eggs:** 4–5; white without markings

**Incubation:** 15–16 days; female incubates

**Fledging:** 15–16 days; male and female feed the young

**Migration:** complete, to Florida, other southern states and Mexico

**Food:** insects

**Compare:** The Gray Catbird (p. 257) has a black crown and a chestnut patch under its tail. The Eastern Phoebe lacks any distinctive markings. Listen for its well-enunciated "fee-bee" call and look for the hawking and tail-pumping behaviors to help identify this bird.

**Stan's Notes:** A sparrow-size bird that often perches on the end of a dead branch. Found in forests, yards and farms. In a process called hawking, it waits for a passing insect. When a bug flies near, it launches out to catch it and then returns to the same branch. It has a distinctive habit of pumping its tail up and down while perching. Builds nest beneath the eaves of houses, under bridges or in other sheltered spots. Uses mud, grass and moss for nest materials and hair (and sometimes feathers) for the lining. The common name is derived from its distinct "fee-bee" call, which it repeats over and over from the top of dead branches.

# Eastern Kingbird
*Tyrannus tyrannus*

SUMMER

**Size:** 8" (20 cm)

**Male:** Mostly gray and black with a white chin and belly. Black head and tail with a distinct white band on the tip of the tail. Concealed red crown, rarely seen.

**Female:** same as male

**Juvenile:** same as adults

**Nest:** cup; male and female build; 1 brood per year

**Eggs:** 3–4; white with brown markings

**Incubation:** 16–18 days; female incubates

**Fledging:** 16–18 days; female and male feed the young

**Migration:** complete, to Mexico and Central America and South America

**Food:** insects, fruit

**Compare:** The American Robin (p. 261) is larger and has a rust-red breast. The Eastern Phoebe (p. 245) is smaller and has an olive-green belly. Look for the white tail band to identify the Kingbird.

**Stan's Notes:** A summer resident in open fields and prairies. As many as 20 birds migrate in a group. Returns to the mating ground in spring, where pairs defend their territory. Seems to be unafraid of other birds and chases larger birds. Given the common name "King" for its bold attitude and behavior. In a hunting technique known as hawking, it perches on a branch and watches for insects, flies out to catch one, and then returns to the same perch. Swoops from perch to perch when hunting. Becomes very vocal during late summer, when family members call back and forth to one another while hunting for insects.

# Great Crested Flycatcher
*Myiarchus crinitus*

YEAR-ROUND
SUMMER

**Size:** 8" (20 cm)

**Male:** Gray head with a prominent crest. Gray back and throat. Yellow from the belly to the base of a reddish-brown tail. Lower bill is yellow at the base.

**Female:** same as male

**Juvenile:** same as adults

**Nest:** cavity; female and male construct; 1 brood per year

**Eggs:** 4–6; white or buff with brown markings

**Incubation:** 13–15 days; female incubates

**Fledging:** 14–21 days; female and male feed the young

**Migration:** complete to non-migrator in Florida

**Food:** insects, fruit

**Compare:** The Eastern Kingbird (p. 247) has a white band across its tail. The Eastern Phoebe (p. 245) is similar, but it lacks a crest and yellow belly. Look for the crest to identify the Flycatcher.

**Stan's Notes:** A common bird of wooded areas in Florida. It lives high up in trees, rarely coming to the ground. Makes long flights from treetop to treetop, moving from one hunting area to another. Gleans insects from tree leaves. Often heard before seen. "Great Crested" refers to the set of extra-long feathers on top of its head (crest), which the bird raises when alert or agitated, like the Northern Cardinal. Nests in an old woodpecker hole but can be attracted with a man-made nest box that has an entrance hole 1½–2½ inches (4–6 cm) in diameter. Often stuffs the cavity with a collection of fur, feathers, string and snake skins.

winter

breeding p. 153

# Sanderling
*Calidris alba*

**Size:** 8" (20 cm)

**Male:** The lightest sandpiper on the beach during winter. Winter plumage has gray head and back and white belly. Black legs and bill. White wing stripe, seen only in flight.

**Female:** same as male

**Juvenile:** spotty black on the head and back with a white belly; black legs and bill

**Nest:** ground; male builds; 1–2 broods per year

**Eggs:** 3–4; greenish olive with brown markings

**Incubation:** 24–30 days; male and female incubate

**Fledging:** 16–17 days; female and male feed the young

**Migration:** complete, to coastal Florida, other southern coastal states, Mexico and Central America

**Food:** insects

**Compare:** Winter Blackbellied Plover (p. 269) has a similar color but is much larger with a larger bill.

**Stan's Notes:** One of the most common shorebirds in Florida, but mostly seen in its gray winter plumage from August to April. Seen in groups on sandy beaches, running out with each retreating wave to feed. Look for a flash of white on the wings when it is in flight. Sometimes a female mates with several males (polyandry), which results in males and the female incubating separate nests. Both sexes perform a distraction display if threatened. Nests on the Arctic Tundra. Rests by standing on one leg and tucking the other into its belly feathers. Often hops away on one leg, moving away from pedestrians on the beach. Surveys show a large decline in numbers since the 1970s.

breeding
p. 155

winter

# Dunlin
*Calidris alpina*

MIGRATION
WINTER

**Size:** 8–9" (20–23 cm)

**Male:** Winter adult has a brownish-gray back with a light-gray chest and white belly. Stout bill curves slightly downward at tip. Black legs.

**Female:** slightly larger than the male, with a longer bill

**Juvenile:** slightly rusty back with a spotty chest

**Nest:** ground; male and female construct; 1 brood per year

**Eggs:** 2–4; olive-buff or blue-green with red-brown markings

**Incubation:** 21–22 days; male incubates during the day, female incubates at night

**Fledging:** 19–21 days; male feeds the young, female often leaves before the young fledge

**Migration:** complete, to coastal Florida, other southern coastal states, Mexico and Central America

**Food:** insects

**Compare:** Winter Sanderling (p. 251) is a similar size, but is lighter and lacks the long down-turned bill.

**Stan's Notes:** Usually seen in gray winter plumage from August to early May. Breeding plumage is more commonly seen in the spring. Flights include heights of up to 100 feet (30 m) with brief gliding alternating with shallow flutters, and a rhythmic, repeating song. Huge flocks fly synchronously, with birds twisting and turning, flashing light and dark undersides. Males tend to fly farther south in winter than females. Winter visitor along the coast. Doesn't nest in Florida.

red morph

gray morph

# Eastern Screech-Owl
*Megascops asio*

YEAR-ROUND

**Size:** 8–10" (20–25 cm); up to 2' wingspan

**Male:** Small "eared" owl that occurs in different colorations. Gray morph is mottled gray and white. Red morph is mottled rust and white. Short wings. Bright-yellow eyes.

**Female:** same as male but slightly larger

**Juvenile:** lighter color than adults of the same morph and usually lacks ear tufts

**Nest:** cavity, old woodpecker cavity or man-made nest box; does not add any nesting material; 1 brood per year

**Eggs:** 4–5; white without markings

**Incubation:** 25–26 days; female incubates, male feeds the female during incubation

**Fledging:** 26–27 days; male and female feed the young

**Migration:** non-migrator; moves around in winter

**Food:** large insects, small mammals, birds, snakes

**Compare:** Burrowing Owl (p. 163) is slightly larger and lacks ear tufts. Eastern Screech-Owl is hard to confuse with its considerably larger cousin, the Great Horned Owl (p. 219).

**Stan's Notes:** Commonly found in forests that have suitable natural cavities for nesting and roosting. Active from dusk to dawn. Usually gives a tremulous, descending trill, like a sound effect in a scary movie. Seldom gives a screeching call. Often seen sunning itself at a nest-box hole during winter. Mates may have a long-term pair bond and may roost together at night. Excellent hearing and eyesight. Flaps rapidly and flies silently. Has winter and summer territories. The gray morph is more common than the red.

YEAR-ROUND
WINTER

# Gray Catbird
*Dumetella carolinensis*

**Size:** 9" (23 cm)

**Male:** Handsome slate-gray bird with a black crown and a long, thin, black bill. Often lifts up its tail, exposing a chestnut patch beneath.

**Female:** same as male

**Juvenile:** same as adults

**Nest:** cup; female and male build; 2 broods per year

**Eggs:** 4–6; blue-green without markings

**Incubation:** 12–13 days; female incubates

**Fledging:** 10–11 days; female and male feed young

**Migration:** complete to non-migrator in Florida

**Food:** insects, occasional fruit; visits suet feeders

**Compare:** The Eastern Phoebe (p. 245) is smaller and has an olive belly. The Eastern Kingbird (p. 247) is similar in size but has a white belly and a white band across its tail. To identify the Gray Catbird, look for the black crown and chestnut patch under the tail.

**Stan's Notes:** A secretive bird, more often heard than seen. The Chippewa Indians gave it a name that means "the bird that cries with grief" due to its raspy call. Called "Catbird" because the sound is like the meowing of a house cat. Often mimics other birds, rarely repeating the same phrases. Found in forest edges, backyards and parks. Builds its nest with small twigs. Nests in thick shrubs and quickly flies back into shrubs if approached. If a cowbird lays an egg in its nest, the catbird will quickly break it and eject it.

# Loggerhead Shrike
*Lanius ludovicianus*

**YEAR-ROUND**

**Size:** 9" (23 cm)

**Male:** Gray head and back and a white chin, breast and belly. Black wings, tail, legs and feet. Black mask across the eyes and a black bill with a hooked tip. White wing patches, seen in flight.

**Female:** same as male

**Juvenile:** dull version of adult

**Nest:** cup; male and female construct; 1–2 broods per year

**Eggs:** 4–7; off-white with dark markings

**Incubation:** 16–17 days; female incubates

**Fledging:** 17–21 days; female and male feed the young

**Migration:** non-migrator in Florida

**Food:** insects, lizards, small mammals, frogs

**Compare:** The Northern Mockingbird (p. 263) has a similar color pattern, but lacks the black mask. The Cedar Waxwing (p. 149) has a black mask, but is a brown bird, not gray and black like the Loggerhead Shrike.

**Stan's Notes:** The Loggerhead is a songbird that acts like a bird of prey. Known for skewering prey on barbed wire fences, thorns and other sharp objects to store or hold still while tearing apart to eat, hence its other common name, Butcher Bird. Feet are too weak to hold the prey it eats. Loggerheads from northern states enter Florida in winter, swelling populations. Breeding bird surveys indicate declining populations in the Great Plains due to pesticides killing its major food source—grasshoppers.

male

female

YEAR-ROUND
WINTER

# American Robin
*Turdus migratorius*

**Size:** 9–11" (23–28 cm)

**Male:** Familiar gray bird with a dark rust-red breast and a nearly black head and tail. White chin with black streaks. White eye-ring.

**Female:** similar to male, with a duller rust-red breast and a gray head

**Juvenile:** similar to female, with a speckled breast and brown back

**Nest:** cup; female builds with help from the male; 2–3 broods per year

**Eggs:** 4–7; pale blue without markings

**Incubation:** 12–14 days; female incubates

**Fledging:** 14–16 days; female and male feed the young

**Migration:** complete, to Florida, other southern states, and Mexico; a small percentage are non-migrators

**Food:** insects, fruit, berries, earthworms

**Compare:** Familiar bird to all. To differentiate the male from the female, compare the nearly black head and rust-red chest of the male with the gray head and duller chest of the female.

**Stan's Notes:** Common winter resident in Florida. City robins sing louder than country robins in order to hear one another over traffic and noise. A robin isn't listening for worms when it turns its head to one side. It is focusing its sight out of one eye to look for dirt moving, which is caused by worms moving. Territorial, often fighting its reflection in a window. Males have dark heads and a brighter red breast than females.

displaying

# Northern Mockingbird
*Mimus polyglottos*

YEAR-ROUND

**Size:** 10" (25 cm)

**Male:** Silvery-gray head and back with a light-gray breast and belly. White wing patches, seen in flight or during display. Tail mostly black with white outer tail feathers. Black bill.

**Female:** same as male

**Juvenile:** dull gray with a heavily streaked breast and a gray bill

**Nest:** cup; female and male construct; 2 broods per year, sometimes more

**Eggs:** 3–5; blue-green with brown markings

**Incubation:** 12–13 days; female incubates

**Fledging:** 11–13 days; female and male feed the young

**Migration:** non-migrator in Florida

**Food:** insects, fruit

**Compare:** Loggerhead Shrike (p. 259) has a similar color pattern, but it is stockier, has a black mask and perches in more-open places. The Gray Catbird (p. 257) is slate gray and lacks wing patches.

**Stan's Notes:** A very animated bird. Performs an elaborate mating dance. Facing each other with heads and tails erect, pairs will run toward each other, flashing their white wing patches, and then retreat to cover nearby. Thought to flash the wing patches to scare up insects when hunting. Sits for long periods on top of shrubs. Imitates other birds (vocal mimicry); hence the common name. Young males often sing at night. Often unafraid of people, allowing for close observation.

# White-winged Dove
*Zenaida asiatica*

YEAR-ROUND

**Size:** 11" (28 cm)

**Male:** Light-gray-to-brown dove. A conspicuous white edge on the wings. Small black dash underneath the cheeks. Vivid blue eye-rings around bright-red eyes. Black wing tips with a white patch across the middle of wings, as seen in flight.

**Female:** same as male

**Juvenile:** similar to adult

**Nest:** platform; female and male build; 2–3 broods per year

**Eggs:** 2–4; white without markings

**Incubation:** 13–14 days; female and male incubate

**Fledging:** 13–16 days; female and male feed young

**Migration:** non-migrator to partial

**Food:** seeds, fruit; will come to seed feeders

**Compare:** Mourning Dove (p. 179) is slightly larger and lacks the white line on closed wings and a white-and-black pattern in flight.

**Stan's Notes:** Very similar to the Mourning Dove in behavior and appearance. Feeds on the ground, pecking at seeds and tiny grains of rock to aid digestion. Parents feed young a regurgitated liquid called crop-milk the first few days of life. Male uses its white-and-black wing coloration to display to mate. May nest alone or in large colonies. Year-round resident in most of Florida, but it is not native, being introduced in the 1950s when captive birds were released near Homestead. Gives a distinctive call, "coo-cuk-ca-roo."

Long-billed
Dowitcher

winter

breeding
p. 171

# Short-billed Dowitcher
*Limnodromus griseus*

YEAR-ROUND
MIGRATION

**Size:** 11" (28 cm)

**Male:** Winter plumage back and wings are gray to light brown and the belly is white. Has a long, straight black bill. Off-white eyebrow stripe. Dull-yellow-to-green legs and feet.

**Female:** same as male

**Juvenile:** similar to winter adult

**Nest:** ground; female and male construct; 1 brood per year

**Eggs:** 3–4; olive-green with dark markings

**Incubation:** 20–21 days; male and female incubate

**Fledging:** 25–27 days; male and female feed the young

**Migration:** complete to non-migrator in Florida

**Food:** insects, snails, worms, leeches, seeds

**Compare:** The winter Black-bellied Plover (p. 269) is similar in size, but it has a tiny bill compared with the Dowitcher's long bill. Winter Willet (p. 277) is larger and has a shorter bill and bold black-and-white wing linings.

**Stan's Notes:** Common year-round resident found along coastal Florida and inland on freshwater lakes and marshes. With a rapid probing action like a sewing machine, it uses its long straight bill to probe deep into sand and mud for insects. Can be seen with the less common Long-billed Dowitcher (see inset), but it is difficult to tell the two apart.

breeding
p. 67

winter

# Black-bellied Plover

*Pluvialis squatarola*

**Size:** 11–12" (28–30 cm)

**Male:** Winter plumage is uniform light gray with a white belly and breast. Faint white eyebrow mark. Black legs and bill.

**Female:** less black on belly and breast than male

**Juvenile:** grayer than adults, with much less black

**Nest:** ground; male and female construct; 1 brood per year

**Eggs:** 3–4; pinkish or greenish with black-brown markings

**Incubation:** 26–27 days; male incubates during the day, female incubates at night

**Fledging:** 35–45 days; male feeds the young, the young learn quickly to feed themselves

**Migration:** complete, to coastal Florida

**Food:** insects

**Compare:** Winter Dunlin (p. 253) has a long down-curved bill. Winter Sanderling (p. 251) has a smaller bill. Winter Spotted Sandpiper (p. 151) has a shorter, thicker bill.

**Stan's Notes:** Males perform a "butterfly" courtship flight to attract females. Female leaves male and young about 12 days after the eggs hatch. Breeds at age 3. A winter resident along the Florida coast. Begins arriving in July and August (fall migration). During flight, in any plumage, displays a white rump and stripe on wings with black axillaries (armpits). Often darts across the ground to grab an insect and run.

soaring

juvenile

# Sharp-shinned Hawk

*Accipiter striatus*

WINTER

**Size:** 10–14" (25–36 cm); up to 2' wingspan

**Male:** Small woodland hawk with a gray back and head and a rust-red chest. Short wings. Long, squared tail and several dark tail bands, with the widest at the end of the tail. Red eyes.

**Female:** same as male but larger

**Juvenile:** same size as adults, with a brown back, heavy streaking on the chest and yellow eyes

**Nest:** platform; female builds; 1 brood per year

**Eggs:** 4–5; white with brown markings

**Incubation:** 32–35 days; female incubates

**Fledging:** 24–27 days; female and male feed the young

**Migration:** complete, to Florida, other southern states, Mexico and Central America

**Food:** birds, small mammals

**Compare:** Cooper's Hawk (p. 279) is larger and has a larger head, a slightly longer neck and a rounded tail. Red-shouldered Hawk (p. 191) is larger, has a reddish head and belly. Look for the squared tail to help identify the Sharp-shinned Hawk.

**Stan's Notes:** A hawk of backyards, parks and woodlands. Seen swooping on birds visiting feeders and chasing them as they flee. Its short wingspan and long tail help it to maneuver through thick stands of trees in pursuit of prey. Calls a loud, high-pitched "kik-kik-kik-kik." Named "Sharp-shinned" for the sharp projection (keel) on the leading edge of its shin. A bird's shin is actually below the ankle (rather than above it, like ours) on the tarsus bone of its foot. In most birds, the tarsus bone is rounded, not sharp.

# Eurasian Collared-Dove
*Streptopelia decaocto*

YEAR-ROUND

**Size:** 12½" (32 cm)

**Male:** Head, neck, breast and belly are gray to tan. Back, wings and tail are slightly darker. Thin black collar with a white border on the nape of the neck. Tail is long and squared.

**Female:** same as male

**Juvenile:** similar to adults

**Nest:** platform; female and male build; 2–3 broods per year

**Eggs:** 3–5; creamy white without markings

**Incubation:** 12–14 days; female and male incubate

**Fledging:** 12–14 days; female and male feed the young

**Migration:** non-migrator

**Food:** seeds; will visit ground and seed feeders

**Compare:** The Mourning Dove (p. 179) is slightly smaller and darker. The Rock Pigeon (p. 275) has colorful iridescent patches. Look for the black collar on the nape and the squared tail to help identify the Eurasian Collared-Dove.

**Stan's Notes:** A non-native bird. Moved into Florida in the early 1980s after inadvertent introduction to the Bahamas. It has been expanding its range across North America and is predicted to spread just like it did through Europe from Asia. Unknown how this "new" bird will affect populations of the native Mourning Dove. Nearly identical to the Ringed Turtle-Dove, a common pet bird. The dark mark on the back of the neck gave rise to the common name. Look for flashes of white in the tail and dark wing tips when it lands or takes off.

# Rock Pigeon
*Columba livia*

YEAR-ROUND

**Size:** 13" (33 cm)

**Male:** No set color pattern. Shades of gray to white with patches of gleaming, iridescent green and blue. Often has a light rump patch.

**Female:** same as male

**Juvenile:** same as adults

**Nest:** platform; female builds; 3–4 broods per year

**Eggs:** 1–2; white without markings

**Incubation:** 18–20 days; female and male incubate

**Fledging:** 25–26 days; female and male feed the young

**Migration:** non-migrator

**Food:** seeds

**Compare:** The Eurasian Collared-Dove (p. 273) has a black collar on the nape. The Mourning Dove (p. 179) is smaller and light brown and lacks the variety of color combinations of the Rock Pigeon.

**Stan's Notes:** Also known as the Domestic Pigeon. Formerly known as the Rock Dove. Introduced to North America from Europe by the early settlers. Most common around cities and barnyards, where it scratches for seeds. One of the few birds with a wide variety of colors, produced by years of selective breeding while in captivity. Parents feed the young a regurgitated liquid known as crop-milk for the first few days of life. One of the few birds that can drink without tilting its head back. Nests under bridges or on buildings, balconies, barns and sheds. Was once thought to be a nuisance in cities and was poisoned. Now, many cities have Peregrine Falcons (p. 283) feeding on Rock Pigeons, which keeps their numbers in check.

breeding
p. 187

displaying

winter

**YEAR-ROUND
WINTER**

# Willet
*Catoptrophorus semipalmatus*

**Size:** 14–16" (36–40 cm)

**Male:** Winter plumage is gray with a white belly. A distinctive black-and-white wing lining pattern, seen in flight or during display. Gray bill and legs.

**Female:** same as male

**Juvenile:** similar to breeding adult, more tan in color

**Nest:** ground; female builds; 1 brood per year

**Eggs:** 3–5; olive-green with dark markings

**Incubation:** 24–28 days; male and female incubate

**Fledging:** unknown days; female and male feed young

**Migration:** non-migrator to complete in coastal Florida

**Food:** insects, small fish, crabs, worms, clams

**Compare:** Winter Short-billed Dowitcher (p. 267) is a similar light gray, but it has a longer bill, yellow-greenish legs and rarely looks up from its constant feeding. Greater Yellowlegs (p. 183) is slightly smaller and has a longer neck and yellow legs. Lesser Yellowlegs (p. 169) is smaller and has yellow legs.

**Stan's Notes:** Common along coastal Florida during winter, with many continuing to migrate along the coast to the coast of South America. It appears a rich, warm brown during the breeding season and rather plain gray during the winter, but it always has a striking black-and-white wing pattern when seen in flight. Uses its black-and-white wing patches to display to its mate. Named after the "pill-will-willet" call it gives during the breeding season. Gives a "kip-kip-kip" alarm call when it takes flight. Nests along the Gulf and East Coasts, in some western states and Canada.

soaring

juvenile

# Cooper's Hawk
*Accipiter cooperii*

YEAR-ROUND
MIGRATION

**Size:** 14–20" (36–51 cm); up to 3' wingspan

**Male:** Medium-size hawk with short wings and a long, rounded tail with several black bands. Slate-gray back, rusty breast, dark wing tips. Gray bill with a bright-yellow spot at the base. Dark-red eyes.

**Female:** similar to male but larger

**Juvenile:** brown back, brown streaking on the breast, bright-yellow eyes

**Nest:** platform; male and female construct; 1 brood per year

**Eggs:** 2–4; greenish with brown markings

**Incubation:** 32–36 days; female and male incubate

**Fledging:** 28–32 days; male and female feed the young

**Migration:** non-migrator to partial; moves to find food in winter

**Food:** small birds, mammals

**Compare:** The Sharp-shinned Hawk (p. 271) is much smaller and lighter gray and has a squared tail. Look for the banded, rounded tail to help identify Cooper's Hawk.

**Stan's Notes:** Found in many habitats, from woodlands to parks and backyards. Stubby wings help it to navigate around trees while it chases small birds. Will ambush prey, flying into heavy brush or even running on the ground in pursuit. Comes to feeders, hunting for birds. Flies with long glides followed by a few quick flaps. Calls a loud, clear "cack-cack-cack-cack." The young have gray eyes that turn bright yellow at 1 year and turn dark red later, after 3–5 years.

in flight

female p. 197

male

in flight

juvenile
in flight

# Snail Kite

*Rostrhamus sociabilis*

YEAR-ROUND

**Size:** 16–18" (40–45 cm); up to 3¾' wingspan

**Male:** Dark gray with black wing tips. White rump and undertail. Black tail with thin white terminal tail band. Red eyes and a hooked, thin black bill with an orange base. Orange legs and feet.

**Female:** overall dark brown, light orange legs and feet; slightly larger than male

**Juvenile:** similar to female; bill is shorter and less hooked than adult bill

**Nest:** platform; male builds; 1 brood per year

**Eggs:** 2–4; white with brown markings

**Incubation:** 26–30 days; female and male incubate

**Fledging:** 23–28 days; male and female feed the young

**Migration:** non-migrator; moves to find food in winter

**Food:** apple snails, turtles

**Compare:** Swallow-tailed Kite (p. 87) has a forked tail and white head and chest. Snail Kite is a habitat specialist and is not seen away from bodies of water.

**Stan's Notes:** Once known as the Everglade Kite. Not very common, with populations restricted to wet habitats that have ample snails. Feeds mostly on the large apple snail. Will take advantage of times of high water levels, when more snails are available. Quickly and easily extricates the entire snail from the shell before swallowing it whole. Litter piles of empty snail shells accumulate below a favorite feeding perch. Also feeds on turtles. Uses its long curved bill to reach inside the turtle shell and extract meat a little bit at a time.

juvenile

in-flight
juvenile

in flight

# Peregrine Falcon
*Falco peregrinus*

MIGRATION
WINTER

**Size:** 16–20" (41–51 cm); up to 3¾' wingspan

**Male:** Dark-gray back and tan-to-white chest. Horizontal bars on belly, legs and undertail. Dark "hood" head marking and wide black mustache. Yellow base of bill and eye-ring. Yellow legs.

**Female:** similar to male but noticeably larger

**Juvenile:** overall darker than adults, with heavy streaking on the chest and belly

**Nest:** ground (scrape) on a cliff edge, tall building, bridge or smokestack; 1 brood per year

**Eggs:** 3–4; white, some with brown markings

**Incubation:** 29–32 days; female and male incubate

**Fledging:** 35–42 days; male and female feed the young

**Migration:** complete, to southern states, Florida

**Food:** birds (Rock Pigeons in cities, shorebirds and waterfowl in rural areas)

**Compare:** The American Kestrel (p. 165) is smaller and has 2 vertical black stripes on its face. Look for the dark "hood" head marking and mustache marks to identify the Peregrine Falcon.

**Stan's Notes:** A wide-bodied raptor that hunts many bird species. The larger females hunt larger prey. Lives in many cities, diving (stooping) on pigeons at speeds of up to 200 mph (322 kph), which knocks them to the ground. Soars with its wings flat, often riding thermals. During courtship, the male brings food to the female and performs aerial displays. Likes to nest on a high ledge or platform for a good view of its territory. A solitary nester and monogamous.

female
p. 211

male

soaring

WINTER

# Northern Harrier
*Circus hudsonius*

**Size:** 18–22" (45–56 cm); up to 4' wingspan

**Male:** Slender, low-flying hawk. Silver-gray with a large white rump patch and white belly. Long tail with faint narrow bands. Black wing tips. Yellow eyes.

**Female:** dark-brown back, brown streaking on breast and belly, large white rump patch, thin black tail bands, black wing tips, yellow eyes

**Juvenile:** similar to female, with an orange breast

**Nest:** ground; female and male construct; 1 brood per year

**Eggs:** 4–8; bluish white without markings

**Incubation:** 31–32 days; female incubates

**Fledging:** 30–35 days; male and female feed the young

**Migration:** complete, to Florida, other southern coastal states, Mexico and Central America

**Food:** mice, snakes, insects, small birds

**Compare:** Slimmer than Red-tailed Hawk (p. 213). Cooper's Hawk (p. 279) has a rusty breast. Look for a low-gliding hawk with a large white rump patch to identify the male Harrier.

**Stan's Notes:** One of the easiest of hawks to identify. Glides just above the ground, following the contours of the land while searching for prey. Holds its wings just above horizontal, tilting back and forth in the wind, similar to Turkey Vultures. Formerly called the Marsh Hawk due to its habit of hunting over marshes. Feeds and nests on the ground. Will also preen and rest on the ground. Unlike other hawks, mainly uses its hearing to find prey, followed by sight. At any age, has a distinctive owl-like face disk.

juvenile

in flight

# Yellow-crowned Night-Heron

*Nyctanassa violacea*

YEAR-ROUND
SUMMER

**Size:** 24" (60 cm); up to 3½' wingspan

**Male:** Stocky gray heron with a black head, white cheek patch and yellow-to-white crown. Thick dark bill. Slender yellow legs. Long, thin white plumes extend from the back of head during breeding season.

**Female:** same as male

**Juvenile:** brown with white streaks and a dark bill, green legs

**Nest:** platform; female and male build; 1 brood per year

**Eggs:** 4–6; light blue without markings

**Incubation:** 21–25 days; female and male incubate

**Fledging:** 21–25 days; female and male feed the young

**Migration:** non-migrator to partial migrator in Florida

**Food:** aquatic insects, fish, crustaceans

**Compare:** One of many heron species in Florida. Great Blue Heron (p. 291) is twice as large, has longer legs and lacks a black chin. The distinctively patterned head makes this heron easy to identify.

**Stan's Notes:** This heron hunts in the evening and early morning, as the common name implies, but it can also be active during the day. Found from coastal mangroves to interior swamps, often hunting fiddler crabs and crayfish. Not uncommon for it to nest in large heron rookeries. Sometimes will nest by itself or in small colonies. Usually seen alone or in small groups. During breeding season, the crown acquires a yellow hue.

in flight

# Canada Goose
*Branta canadensis*

YEAR-ROUND WINTER

**Size:** 25–43" (64–109 cm); up to 5½' wingspan

**Male:** Large gray goose with a black neck and head. White chin and cheek strap.

**Female:** same as male

**Juvenile:** same as adults

**Nest:** platform, on the ground; female builds; 1 brood per year

**Eggs:** 5–10; white without markings

**Incubation:** 25–30 days; female incubates

**Fledging:** 42–55 days; male and female teach the young to feed

**Migration:** non-migrator in Florida

**Food:** aquatic plants, insects, seeds

**Compare:** rarely confused with any other bird

**Stan's Notes:** A year-round resident in parts of Florida. Calls a classic "honk-honk-honk," especially in flight. Flocks fly in a large V when traveling long distances. Begins breeding in the third year. Adults mate for many years. If threatened, they will hiss as a warning. Males stand as sentinels at the edge of their group and will bob their heads and become aggressive if approached. Adults molt their primary flight feathers while raising their young, rendering family groups temporarily flightless. Several subspecies occur in the U.S. Generally eastern groups are paler than western. Their size also varies, decreasing northward. The smallest subspecies is in the Arctic.

in flight

# Great Blue Heron
*Ardea herodias*

**Size:** 42–48" (107–122 cm); up to 6' wingspan

**Male:** Tall and gray. Black eyebrows end in long plumes at the back of the head. Long yellow bill. Long feathers at the base of the neck drop down in a kind of necklace. Long legs.

**Female:** same as male

**Juvenile:** same as adults, but more brown than gray, with a black crown; lacks plumes

**Nest:** platform in a colony; male and female build; 1 brood per year

**Eggs:** 3–5; blue-green without markings

**Incubation:** 27–28 days; female and male incubate

**Fledging:** 56–60 days; male and female feed the young

**Migration:** non-migrator in Florida

**Food:** small fish, frogs, insects, snakes, baby birds

**Compare:** Tricolored Heron (p. 117) is half the size of the Great Blue Heron and has a white belly. The Green Heron (p. 303) is much smaller and has a short neck. The Sandhill Crane (p. 293) has a red cap. Look for the long, yellow bill to help identify the Great Blue Heron.

**Stan's Notes:** One of the most common herons in Florida. Found in open water, from small ponds to large lakes. Stalks small fish in shallow water. Will strike at mice, squirrels and nearly anything it comes across. Red-winged Blackbirds will attack it to stop it from taking their babies out of the nest. In flight, it holds its neck in an S shape and slightly cups its wings, while the legs trail straight out behind. Nests in a colony of up to 100 birds. Nests in trees near or hanging over water. Barks like a dog when startled.

in flight

rusty stain

in-flight rusty stain

# Sandhill Crane
*Grus canadensis*

YEAR-ROUND
MIGRATION
WINTER

**Size:** 42–48" (107–122 cm); up to 7' wingspan

**Male:** Elegant gray crane with long legs and neck. Wings and body often rust brown from mud staining. Scarlet-red cap. Yellow to red eyes.

**Female:** same as male

**Juvenile:** dull brown with yellow eyes; lacks a red cap

**Nest:** ground; female and male construct; 1 brood per year

**Eggs:** 2; olive with brown markings

**Incubation:** 28–32 days; female and male incubate

**Fledging:** 65 days; female and male feed the young

**Migration:** complete to non-migrator in Florida

**Food:** insects, fruit, worms, plants, amphibians

**Compare:** The Great Blue Heron (p. 291) has a longer bill and holds its neck in an S shape during flight. Look for the scarlet-red cap to help identify the Sandhill Crane.

**Stan's Notes:** One of the tallest birds in Florida. Preens mud into its feathers, staining its plumage rust brown (see insets). Gives a very loud and distinctive rattling call, often heard before the bird is seen. Flight is characteristic, with a faster upstroke, making the wings look like they're flicking in flight. Can fly at heights of over 10,000 feet (3,050 m). Found in wetlands and often seen in large, undisturbed fields close to water. Nests on the ground in a large mound of aquatic vegetation. Performs a spectacular mating dance: The birds will face each other, then bow and jump into the air while making loud cackling sounds and flapping their wings. They will also flip sticks and grass into the air during their dance.

male

female

# Ruby-throated Hummingbird

*Archilochus colubris*

**Size:** 3–3½" (7.5–9 cm)

**Male:** Tiny iridescent green bird with black throat patch that reflects bright ruby red in sun.

**Female:** same as male, but lacking the throat patch

**Juvenile:** same as female

**Nest:** cup; female builds; 1–2 broods per year

**Eggs:** 2; white without markings

**Incubation:** 12–14 days; female incubates

**Fledging:** 14–18 days; female feeds the young

**Migration:** complete, to southern Florida, other southern states, Mexico and Central America

**Food:** nectar, insects; will come to nectar feeders

**Compare:** No other bird is as tiny. The Sphinx Moth also hovers at flowers but has clear wings, doesn't hum in flight, moves much slower than the Ruby-throated and can be approached.

**Stan's Notes:** This is the smallest bird in Florida. Can fly straight up, straight down or backward and hover in midair. Does not sing but chatters or buzzes to communicate. Weighs about the same as a U.S. penny; it takes about five average-size hummingbirds to equal the weight of one chickadee. The wings create the humming sound. Flaps 50–60 times or more per second when flying at top speed. Breathes 250 times per minute. Heart beats up to 1,260 times per minute. Builds a stretchy nest with plant material and spiderwebs, gluing pieces of lichen to the exterior for camouflage. Attracted to colorful, tubular flowers. Will extract and eat insects trapped in spiderwebs. A long-distance migrator, some wintering in southern Florida, the rest in the tropics of Central America.

male

female

# Painted Bunting
*Passerina ciris*

SUMMER
MIGRATION
WINTER

**Size:** 5½" (14 cm)

**Male:** An amazing combination of colors. A green back, deep blue head and orange chest and belly. Dark wings and tail.

**Female:** bright green above, light green below

**Juvenile:** drab version of the female with only some small spots of green

**Nest:** cup; female and male construct; 1–2 broods per year

**Eggs:** 3–5; pale blue with brown markings

**Incubation:** 11–12 days; female incubates

**Fledging:** 12–14 days; female and male feed the young

**Migration:** complete, to Florida, other southern states, Bahamas, Cuba, Mexico and Central America

**Food:** seeds, insects; will visit seed feeders

**Compare:** No other bird can compare with the male's striking colors. The female is uniquely green and rarely confused with any other bird.

**Stan's Notes:** A wonderful bunting of backyard gardens, woodland edges and along brushy roads. Visits seed feeders in wooded yards. Well known for its loud, clear and varied warbling phrases. Cup nest, made of grass and lined with animal hair, is usually in a deep, tangled mass of vines. A common cowbird host, this unfortunately often results in it raising the cowbird young and not its own. Although it winters in southern Florida, most continue to migrate southward. Often captured in Central America and sold as a caged bird; both activities are illegal in the U.S. and should not be supported.

# Monk Parakeet
*Myiopsitta monachus*

**Size:** 12" (30 cm)

**Male:** A lime-green back and belly. Gray forehead extending into chest. Tips and trailing edge of wings are blue. A short, hooked yellow bill. Long narrow tail.

**Female:** same as male

**Juvenile:** same as adult

**Nest:** cavity, in a large stick nest; female and male build; 1 brood per year

**Eggs:** 4–6; off-white without markings

**Incubation:** 12–14 days; female incubates

**Fledging:** 28–30 days; female and male feed young

**Migration:** non-migrator

**Food:** fruit, seeds

**Compare:** Several parakeet species occur in Florida, but the Monk Parakeet is the most widespread in southern Florida. Usually seen in urban parks.

**Stan's Notes:** The Monk Parakeet has two toes pointing forward and two toes back. This is unlike most other birds, which have three toes pointing forward and one back. The toe arrangement helps the foot hold food while bringing it to the mouth. Builds a huge colony nest from sticks. There are over 300 parakeet species in the world. The Monk Parakeet, which breeds in southern Florida, is originally from Argentina. The only native North American parakeet was the Carolina Parakeet. Now extinct, it was last reported in Florida in the 1920s. All parakeets currently in Florida came from release or are escaped pets.

female
p. 203

male

# Wood Duck
*Aix sponsa*

YEAR-ROUND
WINTER

**Size:** 17–20" (43–51 cm)

**Male:** Small, highly ornamented dabbling duck. Mostly green head and crest patterned with black and white. Rusty chest and a white belly. Red eyes.

**Female:** brown duck with a bright-white eye-ring, not-so-obvious crest and blue patch on wings (speculum), often hidden

**Juvenile:** similar to female

**Nest:** cavity; female lines an old woodpecker cavity or a nest box in a tree; 1 brood per year

**Eggs:** 10–15; creamy white without markings

**Incubation:** 28–36 days; female incubates

**Fledging:** 56–68 days; female teaches the young to feed

**Migration:** non-migrator to partial in Florida

**Food:** aquatic insects, plants, seeds

**Compare:** Male Northern Shoveler (p. 307) is larger with a long wide bill. Similar in size to male Hooded Merganser (p. 71), which has a crest "hood" it raises to reveal a large white patch.

**Stan's Notes:** A duck of quiet, shallow backwater ponds. Nearly extinct around 1900 due to overhunting, doing well now. Nests in tree cavity or nest box. Seen flying in forests or perching on high branches. Female takes off with a loud squealing call and enters the nest cavity from full flight. Lays some eggs in a neighboring nest (egg dumping), resulting in more than 20 eggs in some clutches. Hatchlings stay in nest for 24 hours, then jump from as high as 60 feet (18 m) to the ground or water to follow their mother. They never return to the nest.

in flight

# Green Heron
*Butorides virescens*

**Size:** 16–22" (41–56 cm)

**Male:** Short and stocky. Blue-green back and rust-red neck and breast. Dark-green crest. Short legs are normally yellow but turn bright orange during the breeding season.

**Female:** same as male

**Juvenile:** similar to adults, with a bluish-gray back and white-streaked breast and neck

**Nest:** platform; female and male build; 2 broods per year

**Eggs:** 2–4; light green without markings

**Incubation:** 21–25 days; female and male incubate

**Fledging:** 35–36 days; female and male feed the young

**Migration:** non-migrator to complete in Florida

**Food:** small fish, aquatic insects, small amphibians

**Compare:** Green Heron is smaller than the Tricolored Heron (p. 117) and lacks the long neck of most other herons. Also much smaller than the Great Blue Heron (p. 291). Look for a small heron with a dark green back and crest to identify the Green.

**Stan's Notes:** Often gives an explosive, rasping "skyew" call when startled. Holds its head close to its body, which sometimes makes it look like it doesn't have a neck. Waits on the shore or wades stealthily, hunting for small fish, aquatic insects and small amphibians. Places an object, such as an insect, on the water's surface to attract fish to catch. Nests in a tall tree, often a short distance from the water. The nest can be very high up in the tree. Babies give a loud ticking sound, like the ticktock of a clock.

female
p. 209

male

YEAR-ROUND

# Mallard
*Anas platyrhynchos*

**Size:** 19–21" (48–53 cm)

**Male:** Large, bulbous green head, white necklace and rust-brown or chestnut chest. Gray-and-white sides. Yellow bill. Orange legs and feet.

**Female:** brown with an orange-and-black bill and blue-and-white wing mark (speculum)

**Juvenile:** same as female but with a yellow bill

**Nest:** ground; female builds; 1 brood per year

**Eggs:** 7–10; greenish to whitish, unmarked

**Incubation:** 26–30 days; female incubates

**Fledging:** 42–52 days; female leads the young to food

**Migration:** non-migrator in Florida

**Food:** seeds, plants, aquatic insects; will come to ground feeders offering corn

**Compare:** Most people recognize this common duck. Male Northern Shoveler (p. 307) has a white chest with rusty sides and a very large, spoon-shaped bill. Look for the green head and yellow bill to identify the male Mallard.

**Stan's Notes:** A familiar dabbling duck of lakes and ponds. Also found in rivers, streams and some backyards. Tips forward to feed on vegetation on the bottom of shallow water. The name "Mallard" comes from the Latin word *masculus*, meaning "male," referring to the male's habit of taking no part in raising the young. Male and female have white underwings and white tails, but only the male has black central tail feathers that curl upward. Unlike the female, the male doesn't quack. Returns to its birthplace each year.

female
p. 207

male

# Northern Shoveler
*Anas clypeata*

WINTER

**Size:** 19–21" (48–53 cm)

**Male:** Medium-sized duck with an iridescent green head, rust sides, white chest. Extraordinarily large, spoon-shaped bill, almost always held pointed toward the water.

**Female:** brown and black all over, green wing patch (speculum) and a large spoon-shaped bill

**Juvenile:** same as female

**Nest:** ground; female builds; 1 brood per year

**Eggs:** 9–12; olive without markings

**Incubation:** 22–25 days; female incubates

**Fledging:** 30–60 days; female leads the young to food

**Migration:** complete, to Florida, other southern states, Mexico and Central America

**Food:** aquatic insects, plants

**Compare:** Male Mallard (p. 305) is similar, but it lacks the large spoon-shaped bill. The male Wood Duck (p. 301) is smaller and has a crest.

**Stan's Notes:** One of several species of shovelers. Called "Shoveler" due to the peculiar, shovel-like shape of its bill. Given the common name "Northern" because it is the only species of these ducks in North America. Seen in shallow wetlands, ponds and small lakes in flocks of 5–10 birds. Flocks fly in tight formation. Swims low in water, pointing its large bill toward the water as if it's too heavy to lift. Usually swims in tight circles while feeding. Feeds mainly by filtering tiny aquatic insects and plants from the surface of the water with its bill. Female gathers plant material and forms it into a nest a short distance from the water. This winter visitor arrives in Florida in September and leaves in April.

female
p. 355

male

# American Redstart
*Setophaga ruticilla*

MIGRATION
WINTER

**Size:** 5" (13 cm)

**Male:** Striking black warbler with orange patches on the sides, wings and tail. White belly.

**Female:** olive brown with yellow patches on the sides, wings and tail, white belly

**Juvenile:** same as female; male attains orange tinges in the second year

**Nest:** cup; female builds; 1 brood per year

**Eggs:** 3–5; off-white with brown markings

**Incubation:** 12 days; female incubates

**Fledging:** 9 days; female and male feed the young

**Migration:** complete, to southern Florida, Mexico, Central America and South America

**Food:** insects, seeds, occasionally berries

**Compare:** The male Baltimore Oriole (p. 311) and male Red-winged Blackbird (p. 29) are much larger. The male American Redstart is the only small black-and-orange bird flitting around the top of trees.

**Stan's Notes:** A common and widespread warbler in the state during spring and fall migration. Found in woodlands, parks and yards and at forest edges. Prefers large, unbroken tracts of forest. Appears hyperactive when it feeds, hovering and darting back and forth to glean insects from leaves. Often droops wings and fans tail before launching out to catch an insect. Look for the flashing black-and-orange colors of the male high up in trees. First-year males have yellow markings and look like the females. Sings a high-pitched song that builds in intensity and then suddenly ends.

female
p. 359

male

# Baltimore Oriole
*Icterus galbula*

MIGRATION
WINTER

**Size:** 7–8" (18–20 cm)

**Male:** Flaming orange with a black head and back. White-and-orange wing bars. Orange-and-black tail. Gray bill and dark eyes.

**Female:** pale yellow with orange tones, gray-brown wings, white wing bars, gray bill, dark eyes

**Juvenile:** same as female

**Nest:** pendulous; female builds; 1 brood per year

**Eggs:** 4–5; bluish with brown markings

**Incubation:** 12–14 days; female incubates

**Fledging:** 12–14 days; female and male feed the young

**Migration:** complete, to Florida, Mexico, Central America and South America

**Food:** insects, fruit, nectar; comes to nectar, orange-half and grape-jelly feeders

**Compare:** The male American Redstart (p. 309) has much less orange. The male Orchard Oriole (p. 313) is much darker orange. Look for the flaming orange to identify the male Baltimore Oriole.

**Stan's Notes:** A fantastic songster, often heard before seen. Easily attracted to a feeder that offers sugar water (nectar), orange halves or grape jelly. Parents bring their young to feeders. Sits at the top of trees, feeding on caterpillars. Female builds a sock-like nest at the outermost branches of tall trees. Prefers parks, yards and forests and often returns to the same area year after year. Young males turn orange-and-black at 1½ years of age. Usually seen during migration and winter.

female
p. 361

male

female
p. 361

first-year
male

# Orchard Oriole
*Icterus spurius*

SUMMER

| | |
|---|---|
| **Size:** | 7–8" (18–20 cm) |
| **Male:** | Dark orange with black head, throat, upper back, wings and tail. White wing bar. Bill is long and thin. Gray mark on lower bill. |
| **Female:** | olive-green back, dull-yellow belly and gray wings with 2 indistinct white wing bars |
| **Juvenile:** | same as female; first-year male looks like the female, with a black bib |
| **Nest:** | pendulous; female builds; 1 brood per year |
| **Eggs:** | 3–5; pale blue to white, brown markings |
| **Incubation:** | 11–12 days; female and male incubate |
| **Fledging:** | 11–14 days; female and male feed the young |
| **Migration:** | complete, to Mexico, Central America and northern South America |
| **Food:** | insects, fruit, nectar; comes to nectar, orange-half and grape-jelly feeders |
| **Compare:** | The male Baltimore Oriole (p. 311) is brighter orange. Look for the dark-orange plumage to identify the male Orchard Oriole. |

**Stan's Notes:** Named "Orchard" for its preference for orchards. Also likes open woods. Eats insects until wild fruit starts to ripen. Often nests alone; sometimes nests in small colonies. Parents bring their young to bird feeding stations after they fledge. Many people don't see these birds at their feeders very much during the summer and think they have left, but the birds are still there, hunting for insects to feed to their young. Summer resident in northern part of Florida. Often migrates in flocks with Baltimore Orioles.

male

female
p. 125

yellow
male

# House Finch
*Haemorhous mexicanus*

YEAR-ROUND

| | |
|---|---|
| **Size:** | 5" (13 cm) |
| **Male:** | Small finch with a red-to-orange face, throat, chest and rump. Brown cap. Brown marking behind eyes. White belly with brown streaks. Brown wings with white streaks. |
| **Female:** | brown with a heavily streaked white chest |
| **Juvenile:** | similar to female |
| **Nest:** | cup, sometimes in cavities; female builds; 2 broods per year |
| **Eggs:** | 4–5; pale blue, lightly marked |
| **Incubation:** | 12–14 days; female incubates |
| **Fledging:** | 15–19 days; female and male feed the young |
| **Migration:** | non-migrator to partial migrator; will move around to find food |
| **Food:** | seeds, fruit, leaf buds; visits seed feeders and feeders that offer grape jelly |
| **Compare:** | The male Purple Finch (p. 317) has a red cap. Look for the brown cap and streaked belly to help identify the male House Finch. |

**Stan's Notes:** Can be a common bird at your feeders. Very social, visiting feeders in small flocks. Likes to nest in hanging flower baskets. Male sings a loud, cheerful warbling song. It was originally introduced to Long Island, New York, from the western U.S. in the 1940s and is now found throughout the country. Suffers from a disease that causes the eyes to crust, resulting in blindness and death. Rarely, males are yellow (inset), perhaps due to poor diet.

female
p. 137

male

# Purple Finch
*Haemorhous purpureus*

**Size:** 6" (15 cm)

**Male:** Raspberry-red head, cap, chest, back and rump. Brownish wings and tail. Large bill.

**Female:** heavily streaked brown-and-white bird with bold white eyebrows

**Juvenile:** same as female

**Nest:** cup; female and male build; 1 brood per year

**Eggs:** 4–5; greenish blue with brown markings

**Incubation:** 12–13 days; female incubates

**Fledging:** 13–14 days; female and male feed the young

**Migration:** irruptive; moves around in winter in search of food

**Food:** seeds, insects, fruit; comes to seed feeders

**Compare:** The male House Finch (p. 315) has a brown cap and a streaked belly. Look for the raspberry cap to help identify the male Purple Finch.

**Stan's Notes:** Usually seen only during the winter in northern Florida, when flocks of Purple Finches leave their homes farther north and move around searching for food. Travels in flocks of up to 50 birds. Visits seed feeders along with House Finches, which makes it hard to tell them apart. Feeds mainly on seeds; ash tree seeds are an important source of food. Found in coniferous forests, mixed woods, woodland edges and suburban backyards. Flies in the typical undulating, up-and-down pattern of finches. Sings a rich, loud song. Gives a distinctive "tic" note only in flight. Male is not purple. The Latin species name *purpureus* means "purple" (or other reddish colors).

female
p. 363

male

# Summer Tanager
*Piranga rubra*

SUMMER
WINTER

**Size:** 8" (20 cm)

**Male:** Bright rosy-red bird with darker red wings.

**Female:** overall yellow with slightly darker wings

**Juvenile:** male has patches of red and green over the entire body, female is same as adult female

**Nest:** cup; female builds; 1–2 broods per year

**Eggs:** 3–5; pale blue with dark markings

**Incubation:** 10–12 days; female incubates

**Fledging:** 12–15 days; female and male feed young

**Migration:** complete, to Florida, Central America and South America

**Food:** insects, fruit

**Compare:** Similar size as the male Northern Cardinal (p. 321), but the male Cardinal has a black mask, large crest and red bill.

**Stan's Notes:** A distinctive bird of woodlands in Florida, especially in mixed pine and oak forests. Due to clearing of land for agriculture, populations have decreased for over a century and especially most recently. Returning to Florida in late March and with young hatching in May, some pairs have two broods per year. Most will leave Florida by November. While fruit makes up some of the diet, most of it consists of insects such as bees and wasps. Summer Tanagers unfortunately seem to be parasitized by Brown-headed Cowbirds more than just about any other nesting bird in Florida.

female
p. 157

male

juvenile

# Northern Cardinal
*Cardinalis cardinalis*

YEAR-ROUND

**Size:** 8–9" (20–23 cm)

**Male:** Red with a black mask that extends from the face to the throat. Large crest and a large red bill.

**Female:** buff-brown with a black mask, large reddish bill, and red tinges on the crest and wings

**Juvenile:** same as female but with a blackish-gray bill

**Nest:** cup; female builds; 2–3 broods per year

**Eggs:** 3–4; bluish white with brown markings

**Incubation:** 12–13 days; female and male incubate

**Fledging:** 9–10 days; female and male feed the young

**Migration:** non-migrator

**Food:** seeds, insects, fruit; comes to seed feeders

**Compare:** Similar size as the male Summer Tanager (p. 319), but the male Tanager is rosy red. Look for the black mask, large crest and red bill to identify the male Northern Cardinal.

**Stan's Notes:** A familiar backyard bird. Seen in a variety of habitats, including parks. Usually likes thick vegetation. One of the few species in which both males and females sing. Can be heard all year. Listen for its "whata-cheer-cheer-cheer" territorial call in spring. Watch for a male feeding a female during courtship. The male also feeds the young of the first brood while the female builds a second nest. Territorial in spring, fighting its own reflection in a window or other reflective surface. Non-territorial in winter, gathering in small flocks of up to 20 birds. Makes short flights from cover to cover, often landing on the ground. *Cardinalis* denotes importance, as represented by the red priestly garments of Catholic cardinals.

juvenile

in flight

# Roseate Spoonbill

*Platalea ajaja*

YEAR-ROUND
SUMMER

**Size:** 30–34" (80 cm); up to 4' wingspan

**Male:** An overall pink bird with red highlights. White neck with a black patch on the back of the head. Heavy, spoon-shaped flat bill. Long red legs.

**Female:** same as male

**Juvenile:** pale version of adult

**Nest:** platform; female and male build; 1 brood per year

**Eggs:** 1–4; olive green with dark markings

**Incubation:** 22–23 days; male and female incubate

**Fledging:** 35–42 days; female and male feed young

**Migration:** partial to non-migrator

**Food:** fish, aquatic insects, snails, worms, leeches

**Compare:** This is an unmistakable bird of Florida. The Roseate Spoonbill is larger than White Ibis (p. 343), which has a long, down-curved orange-to-red bill unlike the heavy flat bill of the Spoonbill.

**Stan's Notes:** A coastal resident of Florida. This bird is making a comeback from devastating hunting pressures in the 1800s for its wing feathers, which were used in women's hats and fans. Now habitat destruction is limiting its numbers. Swings its spoon-shaped bill to sift fish and insects from shallow waters. Usually seen in small flocks. Nests in mixed colonies with herons. Related to the ibises.

in flight

SUMMER

# Least Tern
*Sterna antillarum*

**Size:** 9" (23 cm)

**Male:** A white and gray tern with a black cap and white forehead. White belly. Black wing tips and a short, deeply forked tail, seen in flight. Bill is light orange-yellow with a dark tip. Leg color is the same as the bill.

**Female:** same as male

**Juvenile:** browner version of adult, with a dark bill and partial black cap during first summer

**Nest:** ground; female builds; 1 brood per year

**Eggs:** 1–3; olive-green with dark markings

**Incubation:** 20–22 days; female incubates

**Fledging:** 19–20 days; female teaches young to feed

**Migration:** complete, to South America

**Food:** aquatic insects, fish

**Compare:** Royal Tern (p. 335) is twice the size and has black legs and a large orange-red bill, unlike the Least Tern's smaller, dark-tipped orange-yellow bill. In flight, look for black wing tips and a short, deeply forked tail.

**Stan's Notes:** The smallest tern in North America, the Least Tern is also an endangered species in many North American locations. Killed by the hundreds of thousands in the early 1900s for its feathers. Its decreasing numbers are now due to predators such as cats and dogs and human disturbance while nesting. Nests in large colonies on sandy beaches. Will often hover over intruders in the colony. Hunts small fish and aquatic insects by plunging into water or skimming over the surface. Recognizes mate by distinctive calls.

in flight

WINTER

# Forster's Tern
*Sterna forsteri*

**Size:** 14–15" (36–38 cm); up to 2½' wingspan

**Male:** White and gray tern with a jet-black crown. Leading edge of wings is gray, and trailing edge is white. Characteristic forked tail is long and white. Orange bill with a black tip. Winter plumage lacks the black crown, and the bill becomes nearly entirely black.

**Female:** same as male

**Juvenile:** similar to adults but lacks the black crown

**Nest:** floating platform; female and male build; 1 brood per year

**Eggs:** 3–5; tan to white with brown markings

**Incubation:** 23–24 days; female and male incubate

**Fledging:** 24–26 days; male and female feed the young

**Migration:** complete to Florida, other southern coastal states, Mexico and Central America

**Food:** small fish, insects

**Compare:** Royal Tern (p. 335) is larger and has a larger orange-red bill. Least Tern (p. 325) is smaller and has a lighter orange-yellow bill. Look for a jet-black crown, orange bill with black tip and white tips of wings to help identify Forster's Tern.

**Stan's Notes:** Usually seen in small colonies. Catches small fish by diving into water headfirst. Will catch insects in flight. Constructs a platform nest on floating vegetation. Nests in small colonies in shallow-water marshes. Was named after Johann Reinhold Forster, a German naturalist who traveled with Captain Cook in 1772.

breeding
in flight

breeding

winter
in flight

winter

# Sandwich Tern
*Thalasseus sandvicensis*

YEAR-ROUND

**Size:** 14–15" (36–38 cm)

**Male:** A white-and-gray tern with a narrow black crown. Slender black bill with a pale-yellow tip. Black legs and feet. Bright-white forked tail seen in flight. Winter plumage has incomplete black cap, white forehead.

**Female:** same as male

**Juvenile:** more gray and brown than adult, bill orange before becoming black with pale tip

**Nest:** platform; female and male build; 1 brood per year

**Eggs:** 1–3; pinkish to olive, marked with black-to-brown spots

**Incubation:** 24–25 days; female and male incubate

**Fledging:** 30–35 days; male and female feed the young

**Migration:** non-migrator to complete migrator, to Mexico, Central America and South America

**Food:** small fish, aquatic insects

**Compare:** Royal Tern (p. 335) is larger and has a larger orange-red bill. The Least Tern (p. 325) is smaller and has a light-orange-to-yellow bill. Look for the black legs and pale-yellow tip of bill of the Sandwich Tern.

**Stan's Notes:** Catches small fish by hovering and diving headfirst into the water. Named after the town of Sandwich in County Kent, England, where it was first described. Breeds along the southeastern U.S. coast. Doesn't breed until 3 or 4 years of age. The young leave nest a few days after hatching and gather with other young, called a "creche," and wait for parents to return to feed them.

in flight

breeding

in flight

winter

# Laughing Gull
*Leucophaeus atricilla*

YEAR-ROUND
WINTER

**Size:** 16–17" (40–43 cm); up to 3⅓' wingspan

**Male:** Breeding adult has a black head "hood" and white neck, chest and belly. Slate-gray back and wings with black wing tips. Orange bill. Incomplete white eye-ring. Winter plumage lacks the "hood" and has a black bill.

**Female:** same as male

**Juvenile:** brown throughout, gray sides, lacking the black head and white chest, has a gray bill

**Nest:** ground; male and female construct; 1 brood per year

**Eggs:** 2–4; olive with brown markings

**Incubation:** 18–20 days; female and male incubate

**Fledging:** 30–35 days; male and female feed young

**Migration:** non-migrator to partial in Florida

**Food:** fish, insects, aquatic insects

**Compare:** Ring-billed Gull (p. 333) and Herring Gull (p. 341) are larger. Look for the black head "hood" and slate-gray back and wings of the Laughing Gull.

**Stan's Notes:** This is a three-year gull that starts out mostly brown and gray. The second year it resembles adults but lacks a complete black head "hood." Breeding plumage in the third year. Male tosses its head back and calls to attract a mate. Nests in marshes in large colonies. Nest is a scrape on the ground lined with grass, sticks and rocks. Adults feed young half-digested food. Name comes from its laughing-like call.

in flight

breeding

juvenile

winter

# Ring-billed Gull
*Larus delawarensis*

WINTER

**Size:** 18–20" (45–51 cm); up to 4' wingspan

**Male:** White with gray wings, black wing tips spotted with white, and a white tail, seen in flight (inset). Yellow bill with a black ring near the tip. Yellowish legs and feet. In winter, the back of the head and the nape of the neck are speckled brown.

**Female:** same as male

**Juvenile:** white with brown speckles and a brown tip of tail; mostly dark bill

**Nest:** ground; female and male construct; 1 brood per year

**Eggs:** 2–4; off-white with brown markings

**Incubation:** 20–21 days; female and male incubate

**Fledging:** 20–40 days; female and male feed the young

**Migration:** complete, to Florida, other southern states and Mexico

**Food:** insects, fish; scavenges for food

**Compare:** Laughing Gull (p. 331) has a black head "hood." The Herring Gull (p. 341) has an orange-red mark on its lower bill and pink legs.

**Stan's Notes:** A common gull of garbage dumps and parking lots and extremely common in winter in Florida. One of the most common gulls in the U.S. Hundreds of these birds often flock together. A three-year gull with different plumages in each of its first three years. Attains the ring on its bill after the first winter and adult plumage in the third year. Defends a small area around the nest, usually only a few feet.

winter

in flight

breeding

# Royal Tern
*Sterna maxima*

YEAR-ROUND

**Size:** 20" (50 cm)

**Male:** Gray back and upper surface of wings with white below. Large orange-red bill. Forked tail. Black legs and feet. Breeding plumage has a black cap extending down the nape. Winter plumage has a white forehead and only a partial black cap.

**Female:** same as male

**Juvenile:** dull-white to gray with only a hint of a black cap that rarely extends down the nape

**Nest:** ground; female and male build; 1–2 broods per year

**Eggs:** 1–2; off-white with dark brown markings

**Incubation:** 30–31 days; female and male incubate

**Fledging:** 28–35 days; female and male feed the young

**Migration:** complete to non-migrator, to coastal Florida

**Food:** fish, aquatic insects

**Compare:** Forster's Tern (p. 327) is smaller and has a small black-tipped bill. Least Tern (p. 325) is half the size and has a lighter orange-yellow bill and a shorter forked tail.

**Stan's Notes:** Winter resident along coastal Florida. Nests in large colonies on islands in the Banana River and Tampa Bay, and other places in southern coastal Florida. Lays one egg (rarely two) in a shallow depression on the ground. Like other terns, Royal Terns plunge from heights 40 feet (12 m) and more into the water headfirst to capture fish and aquatic insects. Populations increase during winter with northern migrants.

in flight

# Cattle Egret
*Bubulcus ibis*

YEAR-ROUND
SUMMER

**Size:** 18–22" (45–56 cm); up to 3' wingspan

**Male:** White with orange-buff crest, breast and back. Stocky with a disproportionately large round head. Red-orange bill and legs. Winter plumage is all white with a yellow bill and dark legs.

**Female:** same as male

**Juvenile:** similar to winter adult but with a dark bill

**Nest:** platform; female and male build; 1 brood per year

**Eggs:** 2–5; light blue-green without markings

**Incubation:** 22–26 days; female and male incubate

**Fledging:** 28–30 days; female and male feed the young

**Migration:** partial to non-migrator in Florida; will move around to find food

**Food:** insects, small mammals

**Compare:** Great Egret (p. 345) is about twice as large and has a much longer neck and a much larger bill. White Ibis (p. 343) has a large down-curved bill.

**Stan's Notes:** Came to South America from Africa around 1880, reaching Florida in the 1940s. Often seen singularly in pastures, hunting insects at cow and horse pies by wiggling its neck and head back and forth and from side to side, while holding its body still. Then it stabs at prey and tosses it to the back of its mouth. Frequently attracted to field fires to hunt newly exposed animals and insects. In some years it is found as far as northern-tier states and Canada.

in flight

# Snowy Egret
*Egretta thula*

YEAR-ROUND
SUMMER

**Size:** 22–26" (56–66 cm); up to 3½' wingspan

**Male:** All-white bird with black bill. Black legs. Bright-yellow feet. Long feather plumes on head, neck and back during breeding season.

**Female:** same as male

**Juvenile:** similar to adult, but backs of legs are yellow

**Nest:** platform; female and male build; 1 brood per year

**Eggs:** 3–5; light blue-green without markings

**Incubation:** 20–24 days; female and male incubate

**Fledging:** 28–30 days; female and male feed the young

**Migration:** non-migrator to complete in Florida

**Food:** aquatic insects, small fish

**Compare:** Great Egret (p. 345) is much larger and has a yellow bill and black feet. Juvenile Little Blue Heron (p. 115) is the same size and has a black-tipped gray bill. Look for the black bill and yellow feet of Snowy Egret to help identify.

**Stan's Notes:** Common in wetlands and often seen with other egrets. Colonies may include up to several hundred nests. Nests are low in shrubs 5–10 feet (1.5–3 m) tall or constructs a nest on the ground, usually mixed among other egret and heron nests. Chicks hatch days apart (asynchronous), leading to starvation of last to hatch. Will actively "hunt" prey by moving around quickly, stirring up small fish and aquatic insects with its feet. In the breeding state, a yellow patch at the base of bill and the yellow feet turn orange-red. Was hunted to near extinction in the late 1800s for its feathers.

in flight

breeding

juvenile

winter

# Herring Gull
*Larus argentatus*

WINTER

**Size:** 23–26" (58–66 cm); up to 5' wingspan

**Male:** White with slate-gray wings. Black wing tips with tiny white spots. Yellow bill with an orange-red spot near the tip of the lower bill (mandible). Pinkish legs and feet. Winter plumage has gray speckles on head and neck.

**Female:** same as male

**Juvenile:** mottled brown to gray, with a black bill

**Nest:** ground; female and male construct; 1 brood per year

**Eggs:** 2–3; olive with brown markings

**Incubation:** 24–28 days; female and male incubate

**Fledging:** 35–36 days; female and male feed the young

**Migration:** complete, to coastal Florida, other southern coastal states

**Food:** fish, insects, clams, eggs, baby birds

**Compare:** Ring-billed Gull (p. 333) is smaller and has yellowish legs and feet and a black ring on its bill. Look for the orange-red spot on the bill to help identify the Herring Gull.

**Stan's Notes:** A common gull of large lakes. An opportunistic bird, scavenging for human food in dumpsters, parking lots and other places with garbage. Takes eggs and young from other bird nests. Often drops clams and other shellfish from heights to break the shells and get to the soft interior. Nests in colonies, returning to the same site annually. Lines its nest with grass and seaweed. It takes about four years for the juveniles to obtain adult plumage. Adults have spotted heads during winter.

in flight

juvenile

YEAR-ROUND
SUMMER

# White Ibis
*Eudocimus albus*

**Size:** 23–27" (58–69 cm); up to 3' wingspan

**Male:** All-white bird with a very long, downward-curving orange-to-red bill. Pink facial skin. Color of legs matches the bill color. Black wing tips, seen only in flight.

**Female:** same as male, but smaller; downward curve of bill is less than curve of male bill

**Juvenile:** combination of chocolate-brown and white for the first two years, dull-orange bill

**Nest:** platform; female and male build; 1 brood per year

**Eggs:** 2–3; light blue with dark markings

**Incubation:** 21–23 days; female and male incubate

**Fledging:** 28–35 days; female and male feed the young

**Migration:** non-migrator to partial in Florida

**Food:** aquatic insects, crustaceans, fish

**Compare:** Glossy Ibis (p. 221) is brown. Snowy Egret (p. 339) has a straight black bill and bright-yellow feet. Cattle Egret (p. 337) has a short yellow bill. Wood Stork (p. 93) has a bald dark head and thick bill.

**Stan's Notes:** More common in southern Florida. Prefers fresh water over salt water, with crayfish a big part of its diet. White plumage with black wing tips and a bright orange-to-red down-curved bill make this species easy to identify. Frequently seen flying in groups of 30 or more. Nests in large colonies in well-made stick nests. Hybridized with the non-native all-red Scarlet Ibis (not shown) and produces young in various shades of pink or red.

in flight

# Great Egret
*Ardea alba*

**Size:** 36–40" (91–102 cm); up to 4½' wingspan

**Male:** Tall, thin, all-white bird with a long neck and a long, pointed yellow bill. Black, stilt-like legs and black feet.

**Female:** same as male

**Juvenile:** same as adults

**Nest:** platform; male and female construct; 1 brood per year

**Eggs:** 2–3; light blue without markings

**Incubation:** 23–26 days; female and male incubate

**Fledging:** 43–49 days; female and male feed the young

**Migration:** non-migrator to partial in Florida

**Food:** small fish, aquatic insects, frogs, crayfish

**Compare:** Cattle Egret (p. 337) is about half the size of Great Egret and has a much shorter neck and much smaller bill. The Snowy Egret (p. 339) is much smaller with yellow feet and a black bill. Larger than juvenile Little Blue Heron (p. 115), which has a black-tipped gray bill. White Ibis (p. 343) has a very long, down-curved orange-to-red bill.

YEAR-ROUND
MIGRATION

**Stan's Notes:** Slowly stalks shallow ponds, lakes and wetlands in search of small fish to spear with its long, sharp bill. Gives a loud, dry croak if disturbed or when squabbling for a nest site at the colony. The name "Egret" comes from the French word *aigrette*, meaning "ornamental tufts of plumes." The plumes grow near the tail during the breeding season. Hunted to near extinction in the 1800s and early 1900s for its long plumes, which were used to decorate women's hats. Today, the egret is a protected species.

in flight

# Whooping Crane
*Grus americana*

YEAR-ROUND
MIGRATION
WINTER

**Size:** 51–53" (130–135 cm); up to 7¼' wingspan

**Male:** White bird with a distinctive red crown and red patch just behind the bill (malar mark). Long dark legs. A long, pointed yellow bill. Black wing tips, seen in flight.

**Female:** same as male

**Juvenile:** similar to adult, tan to cinnamon brown, turns white during first winter

**Nest:** ground; female and male construct; 1 brood per year

**Eggs:** 1–3; cream to white with brown markings

**Incubation:** 29–31 days; female and male incubate

**Fledging:** 80–90 days; female and male feed young

**Migration:** complete to non-migrator to northern Florida

**Food:** insects, fruit, fish, small mammals, seeds

**Compare:** Sandhill Crane (p. 293) is gray and lacks the malar mark. American white Pelican (p. 349) is smaller and holds head near body in flight.

**Stan's Notes:** The tallest bird in North America, but weighs only 10–15 pounds (5–7 kg). The Whooper is the rarest of 15 crane species worldwide and one of only two native to North America. An endangered crane with only 15 birds remaining in 1949. Almost always in marshy habitats in family groups of three or more. Can fly up to 50 miles (80 km) per hour. Takes off by running into wind with wings outstretched. Wingspan equal to or slightly larger than Bald Eagle. Matures at 4–6 years and can live 25 years or more. Thought to mate for life. Mated pairs defend territory of 30–50 acres (12–20 ha). Migrates to northern Canada to nest and raise young.

breeding

in flight

chick-feeding
adult

# American White Pelican
*Pelecanus erythrorhynchos*

YEAR-ROUND
MIGRATION
WINTER

**Size:** 60–64" (152–163 cm); up to 9' wingspan

**Male:** Large white pelican with an enormous bright-yellow-to-orange bill. Yellow legs and feet. Black wing tips and trailing edge of wings. Breeding plumage has a bright orange bill, legs and feet. Chick-feeding adult (an adult that is feeding young) has a gray-black crown.

**Female:** same as male

**Juvenile:** duller white than adult, with a brownish head and neck

**Nest:** ground, scraped-out depression rimmed with dirt; female and male build; 1 brood per year

**Eggs:** 1–3; white without markings

**Incubation:** 29–36 days; male and female incubate

**Fledging:** 60–70 days; female and male feed the young

**Migration:** complete, to Florida and Mexico

**Food:** fish

**Compare:** Very similar to the Brown Pelican (p. 225), but is white with a bright-yellow or orange bill. Look for black wing tips in flight.

**Stan's Notes:** Usually in groups on lakes, slow rivers and reservoirs. Doesn't dive to catch fish, like coastal Brown Pelicans. Instead, groups swim and dip their bills simultaneously into water to scoop up fish. Groups fly in a large V, often gliding, followed by simultaneous flapping. Large flocks swirl on columns of rising warm air (thermals) on hot days. Breeding adults typically grow a flat, fibrous plate on the upper bill, which drops off after the eggs hatch. Usually silent; gives short grunts at the nesting colony.

male

winter
male

female

# American Goldfinch
*Spinus tristis*

WINTER

**Size:** 5" (13 cm)

**Male:** Canary-yellow finch with a black forehead and tail. Black wings with white wing bars. White rump. No markings on the chest. Winter male is similar to the female.

**Female:** dull olive-yellow plumage with brown wings; lacks a black forehead

**Juvenile:** same as female

**Nest:** cup; female builds; 1 brood per year

**Eggs:** 4–6; pale blue without markings

**Incubation:** 10–12 days; female incubates

**Fledging:** 11–17 days; female and male feed the young

**Migration:** partial migrator; small flocks of up to 20 birds move around North America to find food

**Food:** seeds, insects; will come to seed feeders

**Compare:** The female House Finch (p. 125) and the female Purple Finch (p. 137) have heavily streaked chests.

**Stan's Notes:** A common backyard resident. Most often found in open fields, scrubby areas and woodlands. Enjoys Nyjer seed in feeders. Lines its nest with the silky down from wild thistle. Almost always in small flocks. Twitters while it flies. Flight is roller coaster-like. Often called Wild Canary due to the male's canary-colored plumage. Male sings a pleasant, high-pitched song. Moves into Florida for the winter starting in November. Can be a common visitor to feeders all winter, leaving in April for northern states.

male

female

# Common Yellowthroat

*Geothlypis trichas*

YEAR-ROUND

**Size:** 5" (13 cm)

**Male:** Olive-brown with a bright-yellow throat and chest, a white belly and a distinctive black mask outlined in white. Long, thin, pointed black bill.

**Female:** similar to male but lacks a black mask

**Juvenile:** same as female

**Nest:** cup; female builds; 2 broods per year

**Eggs:** 3–5; white with brown markings

**Incubation:** 11–12 days; female incubates

**Fledging:** 10–11 days; female and male feed the young

**Migration:** non-migrator in Florida

**Food:** insects

**Compare:** The male American Goldfinch (p. 351) has a black forehead and wings. The Yellow-rumped Warbler (p. 233) only has patches of yellow and lacks the yellow chest of the Yellowthroat.

**Stan's Notes:** A common warbler of open fields and marshes. Sings a cheerful, well-known "witchity-witchity-witchity-witchity" song from deep within tall grasses. Male sings from prominent perches and while he hunts. He performs a curious courtship display, bouncing in and out of tall grass while singing a mating song. Female builds a nest low to the ground. Young remain dependent on their parents longer than most other warblers. A frequent cowbird host.

male
p. 309

female

# American Redstart
*Setophaga ruticilla*

**Size:** 5" (13 cm)

**Female:** Olive-brown warbler with yellow patches on the sides, wings and tail. White belly.

**Male:** black with orange patches on the sides, wings and tail; white belly

**Juvenile:** same as female; male attains orange tinges in the second year

**Nest:** cup; female builds; 1 brood per year

**Eggs:** 3–5; off-white with brown markings

**Incubation:** 12 days; female incubates

**Fledging:** 9 days; female and male feed the young

**Migration:** complete, to southern Florida, Mexico and Central and South America

**Food:** insects, seeds, occasionally berries

**Compare:** The female Yellow-rumped Warbler (p. 233) is similar, but it has a yellow patch on its rump. Look for yellow patches on the sides, wings and tail to help identify the female Redstart.

MIGRATION
WINTER

**Stan's Notes:** A common and widespread warbler in the state during spring and fall migration. Found in woodlands, parks and yards and at forest edges. Prefers large, unbroken tracts of forest. Appears hyperactive when it feeds, hovering and darting back and forth to glean insects from leaves. Often droops wings and fans tail before launching out to catch an insect. Look for the flashing black-and-orange colors of the male high up in trees. First-year males have yellow markings and look like the females. Sings a high-pitched song that builds in intensity and then suddenly ends.

winter

WINTER

# Palm Warbler
*Setophaga palmarum*

**Size:** 5½" (14 cm)

**Male:** Distinctive yellow eyebrows. Yellow throat, belly and undertail. Obvious chestnut cap. Thin chestnut streaks on the sides of the breast. Dark line across dark eyes. Winter plumage similar but duller, often lacking brown cap.

**Female:** same as male

**Juvenile:** same as adult but duller and brown

**Nest:** cup; female builds; 1–2 broods per year

**Eggs:** 4–5; white with brown markings

**Incubation:** 11–12 days; female incubates

**Fledging:** 12–13 days; female and male feed the young

**Migration:** complete, to Florida, the West Indies and Central America

**Food:** insects, fruit

**Compare:** The Yellow-rumped Warbler (p. 233) is similar in size but lacks the yellow throat and belly of the Palm. Look for the yellow eyebrows and chestnut cap of the Palm Warbler.

**Stan's Notes:** One of the most common and abundant warblers in Florida during winter, second only to the Yellow-rumped Warbler. Frequently seen in backyard woodlands during winter. Look for it to wag or bob its tail while gleaning insects from leaves and flowers of trees. One of the few warblers to feed on the ground. Hops rather than walks. Nests at the edges of northern spruce bogs. Recognizes cowbird eggs, which it either rejects from the nest and destroys or buries under a new nest built on top of the old nest and eggs.

male
p. 311

female

# Baltimore Oriole
*Icterus galbula*

MIGRATION
WINTER

**Size:** 7–8" (18–20 cm)

**Female:** Pale yellow with orange tones and gray-brown wings with white wing bars. Gray bill. Dark eyes.

**Male:** flaming orange with a black head and back, white-and-orange wing bars, an orange-and-black tail, a gray bill and dark eyes

**Juvenile:** same as female

**Nest:** pendulous; female builds; 1 brood per year

**Eggs:** 4–5; bluish with brown markings

**Incubation:** 12–14 days; female incubates

**Fledging:** 12–14 days; female and male feed the young

**Migration:** complete, to Florida, Mexico, Central America and South America

**Food:** insects, fruit, nectar; comes to nectar, orange-half and grape-jelly feeders

**Compare:** The female Orchard Oriole (p. 361) has a dull-yellow belly. Look for the gray-brown wings to identify the female Baltimore Oriole.

**Stan's Notes:** A fantastic songster, often heard before seen. Easily attracted to bird feeders that offer sugar water (nectar), orange halves or grape jelly. Parents bring young to feeders. Sits at the top of trees, feeding on caterpillars. Female builds a sock-like nest at the outermost branches of tall trees. Prefers parks, yards and forests and often returns to the same area year after year. Usually seen during migration and winter.

male
p. 313

female

first-year
male

SUMMER

# Orchard Oriole
*Icterus spurius*

**Size:** 7–8" (18–20 cm)

**Female:** Olive-green with a dull-yellow belly. Gray wings with 2 indistinct white wing bars. Long, thin bill with a gray mark on the lower bill.

**Male:** dark orange with black head, throat, upper back, wings and tail; 1 white wing bar

**Juvenile:** same as female; first-year male looks like the female, with a black bib

**Nest:** pendulous; female builds; 1 brood per year

**Eggs:** 3–5; pale blue to white, brown markings

**Incubation:** 11–12 days; female and male incubate

**Fledging:** 11–14 days; female and male feed the young

**Migration:** complete, to Mexico, Central America and northern South America

**Food:** insects, fruit, nectar; comes to nectar, orange-half and grape-jelly feeders

**Compare:** Female Baltimore Oriole (p. 311) is similar, but has orange tones and more distinct wing bars. The female Summer Tanager (p. 363) is mustard-yellow with a larger bill.

**Stan's Notes:** Named "Orchard" for its preference for orchards. Also likes open woods. Eats insects until wild fruit starts to ripen. Often nests alone; sometimes nests in small colonies. Parents bring their young to bird feeding stations after they fledge. Many people don't see these birds at feeders much during the summer and think they have left, but the birds are still there, hunting for insects to feed to their young. Summer resident in the northern part of Florida. Often migrates in flocks with Baltimore Orioles.

male
p. 319

female

# Summer Tanager
*Piranga rubra*

SUMMER
WINTER

**Size:** 8" (20 cm)

**Female:** Some show a faint wash of red, but most females are a mustard-yellow overall with slightly darker wings.

**Male:** bright rosy-red bird with darker red wings

**Juvenile:** male has patches of red and green over the entire body, female is same as adult female

**Nest:** cup; female builds; 1–2 broods per year

**Eggs:** 3–5; pale blue with dark markings

**Incubation:** 10–12 days; female incubates

**Fledging:** 12–15 days; female and male feed young

**Migration:** complete, to Florida, Central America and South America

**Food:** insects, fruit

**Compare:** Female Orchard Oriole (p. 361) and Baltimore Oriole (p. 359) are similar, but they have wing bars. Look for Summer Tanager's lack of wing bars and larger, thicker bill to identify.

**Stan's Notes:** A distinctive bird of woodlands in Florida, especially in mixed pine and oak forests. Due to clearing of land for agriculture, populations have decreased for over a century and especially most recently. Returning to Florida in late March and with young hatching in May, some pairs have two broods per year. Most will leave Florida by November with very few remaining for winter. While fruit makes up some of the diet, most of it consists of insects such as bees and wasps. Summer Tanagers unfortunately seem to be parasitized by Brown-headed Cowbirds more than just about any other nesting bird in Florida.

# Eastern Meadowlark
*Sturnella magna*

YEAR-ROUND

**Size:** 9" (23 cm)

**Male:** Robin-shaped bird with a brown back and yellow chest and belly. V-shaped black necklace. Short tail with white outer tail feathers, best seen when flying away.

**Female:** same as male

**Juvenile:** same as adult

**Nest:** cup, on the ground in dense cover; female builds; 2 broods per year

**Eggs:** 3–5; white with brown markings

**Incubation:** 13–15 days; female incubates

**Fledging:** 11–12 days; female and male feed the young

**Migration:** non-migrator in Florida

**Food:** insects, seeds

**Compare:** This is the only large yellow bird that has a black V mark on the breast.

**Stan's Notes:** A songbird of open grassy country, singing when perched and in flight. Given the name "Meadowlark" because it's a bird of meadows and sings like the larks of Europe. Best known for its wonderful, clear, flute-like whistling song. Often seen perching on fence posts but will quickly dive into tall grass when approached. Sometimes domes its nest with dried grass. Not in the lark family. A member of the blackbird family, related to grackles and orioles.

# BIRDING ON THE INTERNET

Birding online is a great way to discover additional information and learn more about birds. These websites will assist you in your pursuit of birds. Web addresses sometimes change a bit, so if one no longer works, just enter the name of the group into a search engine to track down the new address.

| Site | Address |
| --- | --- |
| Author Stan Tekiela's homepage | naturesmart.com |
| American Birding Association | aba.org |
| Audubon Center for Birds of Prey | cbop.audubon.org |
| Audubon Florida | fl.audubon.org |
| Avian Reconditioning Center | arc4raptors.org |
| Birds of Prey by Accipiter Enterprises | birdsofprey.net |
| The Cornell Lab of Ornithology | birds.cornell.edu |
| eBird | ebird.org |
| Florida Ornithological Society | fosbirds.org |

# CHECKLIST/INDEX BY SPECIES

Use the boxes to check the birds you've seen.

# MORE FOR THE SOUTH BY STAN TEKIELA

## Identification Guides

Birds of Prey of the South Field Guide

The Kids' Guide to Birds of Florida

Mammals of Florida Field Guide

Wildflowers of Florida Field Guide

## Children's Books: Adventure Board Book Series

Floppers & Loppers

Paws & Claws

Peepers & Peekers

Snouts & Sniffers

## Children's Books

C is for Cardinal

Can You Count the Critters?

Critter Litter

## Children's Books: Wildlife Picture Books

Baby Bear Discovers the World

The Cutest Critter

Do Beavers Need Blankets?

Hidden Critters

Jump, Little Wood Ducks

Some Babies Are Wild

Super Animal Powers

What Eats That?

Whose Baby Butt?

Whose Butt?

Whose Track Is That?